DO IT YOURSELF HAPPINESS

T0352156

DO IT YOURSELF HAPPINESS

How to Be Your Own Counselor

By Lee Schnebly, M.Ed.

FISHER BOOKS

Publishers: Helen V. Fisher
Howard W. Fisher
Fred W. Fisher
E. Thomas Monroe

Editor: Judith Schuler

Art Director: Josh Young

Published by Fisher Books
  A member of The
  Perseus Books Group

**Library of Congress
Cataloging-in-publication Data**

Schnebly, Lee, 1932-
Do-it-yourself happiness.

Includes index.
  1. Attitude (Psychology)
  2. Attitude change.
3. Happiness. I. Title.
BF327.S36 1988 158 88-3692
ISBN 1-55561-012-9 (pbk.)

©1988 Fisher Books

Printed in U.S.A.
Printing 10 9 8 7 6 5 4

Books by

Lee Schnebly:

Out of Apples

Do-It-Yourself Happiness

I Do?

Dedication

To my greatest treasure, my family: Larry, Laurie, Lisa, Lindsay and Lyle, who love me and help me grow.

Thanks

Special thanks to Laurie Schnebly for her typing and editing, and to Lisa Schnebly for her photography and consulting.

CONTENTS

CONTENTS

Be Happy;
Be Your Own Counselor!

I don't know how to change a tire.

I learned English, math and history in school, and my mother taught me to cook and sew. At church I learned about God, and a piano teacher taught me how to play. But in the giant universal School of Life, I must have been absent on tire-changing day. That hole in my self-sufficiency crosses my mind each time I strike out on my own to drive to another city. I always decide to learn how to change a tire as soon as my trip is over.

It's not a huge priority in my life because I still haven't done it. I will *only* when the motivation is strong enough.

Like most people, I enjoy learning a new skill, whether it's something I need to know or something that's fun. (Some subjects are both.) The process of learning is available to everyone, regardless of age, health, sex, intelligence or financial status. That means if there's something you don't yet know it's because you haven't learned it yet.

But I still haven't learned to change a tire.

Fortunately I know a mechanic who's willing to trade

car maintenance for counseling. But he and I laughingly admit we feel frustrated by each other's refusal to act on our good advice. I keep telling him he's got to communicate more with his wife. He keeps telling me I've got to change my oil more often. Both of us are typical in our responses to good advice. We ignore it.

Another area in which I sadly lack knowledge is finance. I have a great deal of admiration for friends whose conversation is peppered with comparisons of balanced mutual funds, brokered CDs and index options. For me, managing to balance the checkbook is cause for unbounded joy. Recently a kindhearted friend lent me a giant book on investments. I'm so intimidated by it I haven't gotten past the table of contents.

Knowing something about cars and finance would enhance my life because I believe dependency diminishes the quality of life. The happiest people are the most self-sufficient.

But the fact is, I'm lazy. I don't want to work very hard for the information I lack. I want information that's presented in an easy-to-read, lighthearted way. I want to be able to read it on my patio while I sip iced tea. My favorite history lesson was reading *Gone With The Wind*. As far as I'm concerned, being educated should be gentle and entertaining.

That's why I'm writing this book.

This book is not meant to replace your counselor, if you have one. In fact, counselors are similar to good mechanics. You need a counselor to help you figure out the problems you've been unable to solve yourself. Most people have the innate capacity for improving their life quite dramatically when they have a little information to help them. It's just that most people were never taught these skills in school or any place else.

Not knowing how to fix a flat tire doesn't mean I'm dumb. It's something I never learned. The only difference between my fiscally sound friends and me is their willingness to learn the subject. I'll know I've arrived when I can hop out of my car, whip out the spare tire and confidently exchange it with the flat while I commiserate with my companion about municipal-bond funds!

Skills are skills. Your ability to can peaches or play golf is like my ability to help people get over a depression. They're processes we've learned. Isn't it wonderful each of us can learn almost any skill we want? We can learn some skills simply by reading about them.

I hope you'll enjoy reading this book. It's not a textbook because textbook writing is not a skill I ever wanted to acquire. But it *is* a helpful book.

If you were to come into my office for counseling, we would deal with your problems in the way I describe here. First I'd ask you to tell me about your problems. I'd jot down a few notes describing what you'd like different in your life. How is life not "working" for you? Who are the people you're having difficulty dealing with? How does their behavior make you feel? What have you tried? What have been the results? How would your life be different if you didn't have these problems?

If I were your counselor, I'd spend our first session getting as much information as I could about your problems. Then I'd have a good grasp of what you want to see changed. In the beginning, I'd be 90% responsible for the work because I have to ask questions and formulate ideas that might help you. Your 10% would be to express yourself and your feelings.

As we continued in the counseling process, the percentage of responsibility would shift. I would continue teaching concepts, ideas and skills. You would continue learning them. Eventually *you* would be 90% responsible for the changes you want to make. My responsibility would shrink to only 10% as I listen, encourage and make minor suggestions. Ultimately, you would be 100% responsible for your life decisions, behavior and consequential happiness or unhappiness.

Sometimes I meet a former client in the grocery store and he or she gives me a hug and says, "You helped me *so much!*" I accept only 5% of the credit. Conversely, I take only 5% of the blame if the person is still unhappy. I can be the teacher of skills, but the client himself uses them or rejects them. So he deserves the lion's share of pride as he sees his life improve. Without his efforts, his life wouldn't change one bit.

Usually during our second visit, I begin the "lifestyle" technique this book is all about. In the following chapters, I explain the process as I would if we were sitting in the chairs in my office. There are a few places I ask you to write down some things about your childhood, just as I would if we were together (except I'd do the writing while you talked).

Then I study your answers for insights to share with you at our next visit. I make notes of my interpretations and make a copy for you. The next time we would discuss them together.

In this book is everything that's involved with the counseling process except me. I've explained the entire process so you won't even miss me. You'll learn the same techniques you'd learn if you were getting a master's degree in counseling and guidance. Maybe not *all* the techniques but some of the best ones. You probably don't *want* a degree in counseling and guidance any more than I want to learn everything about cars. I just want to be able to change a flat tire!

The book will give you specific things to look for as you remember some of your childhood experiences. It will provide you with "new glasses" through which to look at life. You'll enjoy recalling the incidents. Even bad recollections will take on a positive aspect in helping you understand your present attitudes and beliefs.

If you already have a counselor or therapist, you may find some new information to help him or her be even more effective. You may decide you like your lifestyle just the way it is. That's a wonderful awareness! If you're happy, you may not want to rock the boat.

But nearly everyone has at least a few areas that could use improving. Hopefully the following pages will help you find ways of doing that and of enjoying the process!

So here we go. Take a minute to think of some problem you'd like to work on. Keep it in mind as you discover new insights that apply to you. Make some notes if you like, or mentally tuck away the things you learn as you go. By the time you've finished the last page, you'll have just about all the knowledge you need to be your own counselor and create your own happiness!

Chapter 1

No Two
Belief Systems
Are Alike

How often do you shake your head in wonder when someone you love feels differently from the way you feel? Whether it's about important issues, like politics, religion and values, or relatively minor, like the radio station they listen to, it seems we're constantly amazed at the difference in tastes, priorities and preferences.

Driving over a high bridge makes my palms damp. If it's a long bridge, I may even have a mild anxiety attack. I'm the object of scorn to my San Francisco friend, whom I once asked, "How often do you have to go over the bridge?" She looked at me with disbelief and answered, "I *get* to go over it several times a week!"

All the things you enjoy, and the things you loathe, have their origins in your *belief system*. It's the very heart of your personality.

Your individual beliefs are unique to you. Frequently you take them so much for granted that you're unaware of them. Yet every single action you do—every word you speak, every thought and feeling you have—is a direct result of your private belief system.

You have carefully chosen and developed your specific set of beliefs since birth. As a baby in a crib, you looked around and watched life happen. You decided what life was all about. You observed every detail of people's behavior and drew important, although often mistaken, conclusions. By the time you were 5, you already had a long mental list that began with the phrase "Life is a place where . . ."

Some of your beliefs might have been—
Life is a place where . . .

- I must always be good so people will like me.
- people should do whatever I want.
- I have to keep trying to do better.
- men are nice, but women aren't.
- women are good, and men are mean.
- I can't win.
- everybody's out of step but me.
- I'd better not tell the truth.

And so on, ad infinitum. We all have endless lists. We keep them clutched to our hearts, often with a fierce determination that defies anyone's efforts to change us.

It's easy to understand why happy people want to hold onto their beliefs about life. They have a set of attitudes and expectations that work well for them. But it's amazing how determined a person can be to keep his beliefs exactly as he created them many years ago, even if they keep him from being happy. Though someone may be miserable with the way life is treating him, he doesn't want to change.

People especially don't want to change themselves! They want *other* people to change. Most insist (either out loud or silently) that life would be fine "if only . . ."

- ❧ my husband would communicate more . . .
- ❧ my kids would cooperate . . .
- ❧ my in-laws did things right . . .
- ❧ my wife were more affectionate . . .
- ❧ the schools taught like they used to . . .

You may spend a great deal of energy wishing and hoping these things come to pass. Many people waste a lot of time telling others how to change their behavior, thoughts and attitudes. And they continue to feel endless frustration as they cling tenaciously to their peculiar belief systems.

"Why won't they see what I tell them is true?"

"I've told him a million times what he needs to do, and he still doesn't listen!"

"If she had any sense, she'd take my suggestion."

"How do you get people to do what you want them to do?"

We all struggle constantly. I impress myself with my tenacity in holding onto old, foolish beliefs that complicate my life. Millions of times I've expected something to happen a certain way and have been disappointed. But do I want to change my expectation? Nope. That's the way it should be, and that's how I'm going to continue wanting it to be. If it doesn't work that way, I'll keep getting upset about it, if it takes forever!

Besides, I'm good at getting upset over it by now. Why should I stop? I learned as a child that *others* are wrong, not me. This reminds me of a saying my husband heard that we chuckle over—"Hell is *other* people."

Unless parents were happy and well-adjusted, most people learned an unhealthy way of looking at life. "If I'm unhappy, it must be somebody's fault, and they ought to change!" Few people were fortunate enough to learn early that everyone makes his or her own happiness or unhappiness. Most learned to depend on others. They gave themselves permission to blame others when things weren't the way they wanted.

Believing others are responsible for your feelings is a mistaken belief. It's one belief you can change if your life isn't as good as you'd like it to be.

Most Beliefs Are Good

Of all the beliefs you've formed, most are pretty good. Perhaps 90% of them serve you very well, and you'd be foolish to change them.

"People shouldn't lie, cheat or steal."

"People should love each other."

"Work and play are beneficial."

Millions of other healthy beliefs have proved themselves through the years. It's handy you don't have to change those!

But most people have *some* beliefs that mess up their chances at happiness. They'd consider changing these beliefs if they were aware of them. Maybe 5 or 10% of your beliefs were totally erroneous from the very day you formed them. Other beliefs were appropriate *then* but have outlived their usefulness. "I shouldn't go near the stove" was a useful belief at age 2. But you gladly let go of it when your mother said you were old enough to bake cookies.

It's easy to let go of beliefs if you see a benefit. But there are some beliefs you hang onto in spite of the pain they cause you because you don't realize the positive results you'd experience by letting them go. Or perhaps they're so deep within your subconscious mind you're unaware they *are* your beliefs.

Your beliefs are familiar and comfortable to you. You probably couldn't understand why I have the beliefs I've chosen. Even if you knew me very well, you'd be unaware of all the things I believe, partly because I'm unaware of many of my own beliefs. And I'm so used to my own beliefs that yours may be incomprehensible to me.

It's amazing that human beings get along with each other as well as we do, considering how differently we view life. We owe ourselves hearty pats on the backs for managing to coexist somewhat cooperatively when we realize how vastly complex everyone's belief systems are and how different they are from everyone else's.

Belief Systems Are Powerful

As different as they all are, belief systems work in very powerful ways. You can understand someone's behavior when you see it in the context of their belief system, even though that system may be faulty.

Suppose you punish your child when he confesses he did something wrong. He may decide lying makes life easier for him. If he has good sense, he'll probably try lying the next time to see if it works. If he gets away with it and it seems to solve his problems, his belief might become "the best way to keep out of trouble is to lie." But if lying gets him into worse trouble, he may decide "lying causes more trouble than it's worth. I'd better avoid it." The belief he forms in childhood is probably the one he'll respond to when things get shaky in adulthood.

If Patty believes in lying, she'll put a lot of effort into perfecting that skill. She might be an expert at it by adulthood. In fact, lying might have helped her out of some tough spots in her life. She sees it as a good and necessary friend.

Now if I try to get Patty to stop that habit, she's going to look with disbelief at my stupidity. I'm asking her to abandon something she sees as good! If lying is her thing, she'll probably nod soberly and say, "You're right, Lee. I've told my last lie. From now on, I'll always tell the truth," while she watches my face to see if I'm dumb enough to swallow that.

What started as the solution becomes the problem. Pretty soon nobody believes Patty or trusts her. Even then she might steadfastly cling to her belief that lying is a good technique in solving problems. She won't begin to try to change her belief unless she decides it is advantageous for her.

Many have trouble making changes because they're not really conscious of what strong beliefs lie behind habits. One very common mistaken belief I still struggle with is, "If you worry about it, maybe it won't happen."

I'm sure my mother never thought of worry as a preventive measure. It was a habit she picked up from *her* mother. "You just can't help worrying!" she would have explained plaintively, if asked why she did it. "Mothers just do!" She would have defended the practice vehemently as something she couldn't help. In fact, many mothers consciously or unconsciously see worry as a noble endeavor. The more you worry, the better mother you must be!

When our daughter, Laurie, got diabetes at age 3, I was a nervous wreck. I paced the floor, wrung my hands and could neither eat nor sleep. I did everything one instinctively knows one should do when one is a skilled worrier. My mother even got on a train and came to visit so she could worry with me. Goodness knows we were a great team, having worried together through thick and thin for many years. We sat with Laurie in her hospital room, taking turns reading to her and playing with her. We tried to look cheerful and brave for her sake. But we caught each other's eye from time to time with just the right expression to reassure each other we were still worrying!

One day Laurie's doctor looked at me with concern. He suggested I take some tranquilizers to help me through. I firmly declined. I laugh now when I remember his amused remark, "Why not? Are you afraid you might not worry?" At the time I thought he was an insensitive clod, but I have come to see there was some truth to his accusation.

It was a good 30 years before I learned the belief that lay behind the worry habit. "If I worry long enough and hard enough, I might keep it from happening." Only recently did I realize the positive reinforcement involved in worrying. Most of the things we worry about don't come to pass, so there is an unconscious reward to keep doing it.

Larry tells about the man who always wore a big yellow whistle on a chain around his neck. When asked why, he said, "I wear it to keep the elephants away."

"There's not an elephant for miles around here," his companion protested.

The man observed triumphantly, "See? It works!"

So worry works for many of us. We worry about many things that never happen. We unconsciously believe we've got a sure thing going. We refuse to give it up for all the tea in China. After all, Laurie's still alive and healthy, isn't she? Or so I can reason to myself.

Unless I see worrying as the result of a mistaken belief that only complicates my life, I'm going to keep doing it forever. But if I recognize the "magic" I've subscribed to and come to see the advantage of letting it go, I might decide I'm willing to replace that belief with a new one. My new belief might be "I will do all I can to solve a problem, but I will not waste energy on worry!"

Information on ways to go about making that newly changed belief *stick* begins on page 117. For now let's further explore the process of discovering exactly what beliefs (valid and mistaken) you've chosen.

Lifestyle Questionnaire

An instrument called a *lifestyle questionnaire* helps uncover a person's beliefs. I explain to my clients this process enables me to give them an educated guess as to how they see life. By the time we finish, they have a list of statements beginning with "Life is a place where . . ."

The client is the final judge of how valid the proposed beliefs are. But most of the time I'm fairly accurate in my assessment. We discuss each belief together, deciding first whether or not the client really thinks that way. People usually know immediately if the belief is a help or hindrance to them. They can quickly decide which beliefs cause distress in their lives.

However, some beliefs aren't so easy to let go of. One of the most common has to do with perfection. Many people (especially firstborns) believe they should try at all times to be perfect. Getting them to even *consider* imperfection is a real challenge. You can imagine the moral battle going on inside their heads as they think about the premise.

The man who tries to do everything perfectly usually is suffering *some* discomfort in his life, or he wouldn't be in my counseling office. Often it becomes clear, after we do the lifestyle questionnaire, his desire for perfection in himself and/or others is a big problem in his life.

Many times he recognizes it as distressing. Yet he is reluctant to change his belief. He may feel almost sinful at the thought of changing. So we discuss ways his quest for perfection affects his life, his family and his friends. I leave the decision up to him. Frequently he'll consider changing the belief a little bit, perhaps to "It's OK to be imperfect about unimportant things." That's a step in the right direction.

Whether or not you believe perfection is required or worry is necessary, you have beliefs that are open to positive change. With this book, you can become your own counselor. Use the lifestyle questionnaire that follows to determine your own beliefs.

Take time to fill out the questionnaire now, before you finish the book. I say that knowing full well if *I* were reading this book I would never stop and fill anything out, even if the author advised me to. When I want to read, I want to read! I would probably glance at the questions and intend to come back and answer them after I'd finished the book.

The only advantage to filling it out now rather than later is your answers might be more spontaneous now. If you answer them after you read the book, you already know how to interpret them. Sometimes we unconsciously change answers to "doctor them up" a little for better effect.

Fill out the lifestyle questionnaire using a separate sheet(s) of paper. Keep it handy so you can refer to it.

LIFESTYLE QUESTIONNAIRE

1. List the names and present ages of your parents and siblings in the order of their birth. Include any who died and at what age. Write three words describing each one the way you saw him when you were a child.

Name	Age	Descriptive Adjectives
Dad		
Mom		

If more space is needed use a separate sheet of paper.

2. Of your parents and siblings, which one was or is most like you?
   In what ways?

3. Which one was most different from you?
   In what ways?

4. As a small child, how did you go about getting your way?

5. What kinds of compliments did you receive as a child from the people with whom you associated most: parents, teachers, family, friends?

6. What kinds of negative criticism did you receive?
7. When you die (at 100, at least!) what short, descriptive phrase would you like on your tombstone to describe you as you'd *like* to be remembered?
8. If your mother had a sign over the kitchen sink to teach a strong value of hers, what would it have said?
9. What would your father's sign have said?
10. What was your favorite childhood story, book or fairy tale?

What was your favorite part of that story?

With whom did you identify?

11. If you had to come back in another life as an animal, what would you choose to be? Why?
12. If you could wave a magic wand and change anything or anyone about your childhood, what would you change?
13. With that same magic wand, what or whom would you change about your life right now?
14. What problems did you have in your childhood that you still have now?
15. Picture the house you lived in when you were a child. Imagine yourself playing in some secluded spot by yourself. Try to remember a specific place and actually "see" yourself there right now . . . perhaps in your bedroom, in a tree, behind a bush or out in the barn. Imagine yourself where you used to be as a child. Now picture two people who were important to you then—parents, friends, grandparents; any two you want to choose.

What two people do you picture?

Imagine you hear them talking about you, although they don't know you can hear them. Imagine their conversation. One of them says:

The other responds:

What thought do you think to yourself, overhearing

their remarks?

And what feeling (one word) do you feel?

16. What is your earliest memory? It needs to be a *specific* incident, though it needn't be particularly important. Not a general memory, like, "We used to go to Grandma's every Christmas," but rather one incident such as "One day I was sitting on the front step when I saw the ice-cream truck coming down the street. I asked my daddy if I could have some ice cream, and he . . . etc."

17. Now describe five more specific incidents you remember from childhood. All should be memories of events in your life between the ages of 2 and 12.

Begin with the memory of one of the best things that happened to you as a child.

Then one of the worst things you experienced.

Write down an incident from kindergarten or grade school.

Describe another experience, good or bad, about anything.

Describe another experience, good or bad, trivial or important.

These six early recollections are enough, but if you're getting into it and thinking of more incidents, feel free to write down as many as you want. There is no limit.

Now you have completed the lifestyle questionnaire that you will interpret later.

Chapter 2

The Importance
of
Birth Order

Nearly every parent who has more than one child has said on occasion, "I can't understand how they can be so different!" Whether or not you're a parent, if you have brothers and sisters you may have noticed the same thing when you compared yourself with your siblings.

Families may unconsciously label members as they become aware of particular traits and tendencies. "Megan is our helper. Erik is the most sensitive. Kate is such a rebel!" If there were 15 children in a family, there would probably be 15 distinct personality descriptions. Why is that so? The answer is simple and universal. *We all need to feel like we count*.

The need is there at birth, and the process of filling that need begins in the crib. Every baby born is aware on some level of his own inferiority. He begins striving to reverse that feeling, working to feel significant instead. No one likes feeling helpless and dependent. The human condition is one of continuous striving for self-improvement

13

and mastery of some sort.

In infancy, with the goal to "be somebody" already in working order, your personality traits begin to emerge. You discover a simple process—what works best for you is what you'll keep. What doesn't work, you'll discard.

Alfred Adler taught us in the life pattern of every child is the imprint of his position in the family. A child's place in the family constellation influences much of his future attitude toward life.

Firstborn

Let's look at a newborn baby named Jason. Assuming his parents are like most parents, they are delighted beyond words with this amazing offspring! They watch him with fascination; they laugh at his antics. They thrill at his first smile, his first step, his first word. This is the Child of the Century. They worry if he coughs or stumbles, and they praise him when he goes in the potty. They hover constantly. Jason correctly assumes he is the center of the universe. He is the most important thing that ever happened to his parents.

Along with their delight, however, they feel a huge sense of responsibility to form this baby into a Perfect Human Being. So they set standards for him they will never set for any subsequent children. They begin to teach Jason perfection. The first child has a tough row to hoe, faced with totally unrealistic expectations from unreasonably idealistic parents.

By the trial-and-error method, Jason learns if he's good he gets love and approval. If he's bad, he gets hurtful disapproval. Most first children decide to "be good." They get proficient at pleasing and at being responsible, reliable and dependable. They love hearing their parents brag about their good grades in kindergarten. They get the hang of their role in life down pat. Everyone in the house behaves predictably until . . . (if books had sound effects you would hear ominous music and thunder at this point) the second child is born. Woe to the firstborn who must give up his throne. He is the only child in the family who is ever "dethroned." No subsequent child ever experiences being the center of the universe, so they never know the pain that comes with having to give up that prominent position.

We can safely assume Jason is doomed to spend the rest of his life looking back over his shoulder to see if that second child is catching up with him. *His motto is "I was here first, and first I'll stay."*

Second Child

Whether the second child is the same sex or not has a lot of bearing on both children's belief systems. But the second child's arrival is certain to have a profound effect.

Another important variable is the time lapse between the two births. If the children are less than 4 years apart, they're both likely to follow a predictable pattern in personality development. A gap of more than 4 years means each sibling's life is affected by the other but with less impact than if they were born closer together.

Jason, as our first child, will make a decision in the next few years that will affect his entire future. How can he continue to be Number 1? Many first children find they *can* continue their behavior of being smart, good, pleasing, superior and responsible. They may be able to do it so well the second child is unable to come close to matching it. The second child will look in other directions for *his* claim to fame.

But if the oldest discovers his former behavior no longer works, he'll cast about for new techniques to make him Number 1 at getting attention in his family. Let's say Number 2 has the audacity to try being smart, good, pleasing, superior and responsible. If Jason finds his position threatened, he may decide, "If I can't be the best kid in the family, I'll be the best at being the *worst* kid."

Let's call the second child Emily and look at her thought process. She knows she's got her work cut out for her if she's going to beat Jason. She will bring boundless determination to her early decision to catch up with Jason and surpass him if it is humanly possible. And the intensity of her effort deserves admiration, although certainly not from Jason!

From Emily's point of view, Jason wears several hats. First, he is her playmate and perhaps her protector and teacher of sorts. But he's also bigger, stronger, more capable and seemingly better than she. That's hard to swallow.

Emily will begin to look for ways *she* can be "better." Usually it's clear to her which areas to avoid—the ones in which Jason is the most skilled, in which he is already the recognized "champ." Instinctively she bypasses those and seeks out different arenas in which to polish and demonstrate her worthiness. If he is quiet, she'll be noisy. If he's studious, she'll be the social butterfly. If he's shy, it's amazing how outgoing she'll become! Rarely does the second child compete in the first's fields of expertise, but she tries to outdo him in other ways.

Our second child, Lisa, was a waitress during her college years. She reported her boss' lecture to all the waitresses one evening. "I want all of you to stand straight. Have good posture when you're working. Look at Lisa; she has great posture."

Lisa hastened to explain, "That's because I'm a second child. I've spent my whole life trying to be taller than Laurie."

Interestingly, she *is* taller. That little story began my awareness of how many second children are taller than their older siblings. I can't quite believe it's done by sheer determination to surpass, yet I find myself wondering.

Emily is continuously aware of someone in front of her who is more advanced in everything he does. She often acts as if she were in a race and may be hyperactive and pushy. *Her second-child motto is "I must try harder."* Though that lifestyle begins as she tries to gain importance and recognition within the family circle, it becomes a lifetime decision. It accompanies Emily forever as she presses onward to achieve, accomplish, impress, surpass, often relentlessly driving herself without ever knowing why.

Tough as it is for Jason and Emily, it's even tougher for two siblings of the same sex. Two girls or two boys share so many of the same goals and desires that the competition can be fierce. In spite of the strong bond and genuine caring they may feel, their competition colors thousands of their decisions during their formative years. During this time goals are chosen, tested and retained or rejected according to the success experienced.

Our first child, Laurie, was typical in her "goodness," her obedience and her desire to be responsible and pleasing to us and everyone she met. She strove for perfection, and we rewarded her efforts with lavish praise. Our standards for Laurie were much higher than they were for our other children. She did her best to measure up to them.

When Lisa was born, 19 months later, it didn't take her long to find out Laurie was way ahead in being able to do "everything" well. To Lisa it must have seemed an impossible task to attempt to be as socially skilled and adept at pleasing as Laurie, though I suspect she may have tried a few times. Being constantly outshone by someone else has a predictable effect. It wasn't long before Lisa gave up that behavior for a technique that seemed to work better.

We were head residents in a boys' college dormitory when the girls were very small. It was fun watching them respond to the young men who lived there. Laurie stood outside our office smiling at everyone. They'd stop and talk to her a few minutes on their way in and out. Lisa sat nearby in her playpen or walker and watched them go by. If one came up to her to talk, she'd shake her head vigorously, look angry and without saying a word, convey a strong "Get lost, Buster" message.

The boys laughed. One of them said, "I can't wait till she can talk so I can hear what she has to say. I bet she'll cuss me out." Laurie would look agreeably amused at her quaint but obviously inferior sister and smile her way into the boys' hearts.

We can expect opposites in the second child if he is born fewer than 4 years apart. When I was learning these concepts in a class from Dr. Oscar Christensen, he asked who had an older sibling within that age range. I raised my hand proudly. (I adore my older brother, Paul.)

"Describe Paul in three words," he said. Without much time to think about it I offered, "He's studious, conservative and religious."

"Then I would bet you are not studious, not conservative and not religious," he suggested. I was amazed to realize he was right. When we were growing up, everybody knew Paul was "the smart one." I got good enough grades but not the straight A's he did. I put my efforts into playing the piano, being artistic and playing with friends. While my relationship with God is warm and prayerful,

I'm not the churchgoer Paul is. He goes to *daily* Mass and loves every minute of it. He is far more traditional in his thinking than I and is conservative in his clothes and in his lifestyle. I'm not a flamboyant rebel, but compared to him, I lean in that direction.

It's surprising how often the three adjectives describing first and second children are opposites. Not 100% of the time, of course, but often enough to make guessing relatively non-risky. I often ask clients the same question Christensen asked me. If I hear, "Quiet, stingy and a loner," I don't hesitate to guess, "I bet you're noisy, generous and outgoing." More often than not I'm right.

Middle Child

Now if a third child is born, everybody shifts in some way, particularly the second child. She no longer has the distinction of being the youngest. It isn't easy giving up that spot to the new intruder. Alas, the second child becomes the *middle child*. Middle children often feel squeezed. They must cope with the rival they've competed with for their entire lives who's still ahead of them doing more important things. Now their lives are further complicated by the Baby.

They get a taste of what the first child felt when he was dethroned, but with less intensity. They've never had Mom's and Dad's undivided attention. But giving up one's Baby role is never easy. Emily may become discouraged as she tries to find her place of significance in the family. She watches Jason become more responsible after the birth of the new baby and hears Mom say things like, "Jason is a big help to me; he's such a good boy. I can depend on him for anything." And Emily sighs.

She brings Mom a book to read her and hears instead,

"Not now, sweetie. I have to feed the baby." *A middle child's motto is "life is unfair."* She may feel unloved and abused. She may develop some negative behavior to get attention. Even negative attention is better than no attention at all. If it works for her, she may keep it. But if the payoff isn't there, she'll discard it. She tries many different ways to find her important spot and in the process develops some worthwhile skills.

Christensen says, "We learn on the first child. We spoil the baby. Often the middles turn out to be the most well-adjusted." (He is also quick to warn, however, we can never make a statement like that with positive assurance. We can make educated guesses, but we can't say for certain "middles are the best adjusted" or "firsts are always responsible." As human beings, we're far too creative to be labeled and pigeonholed that predictably.)

Nonetheless, birth order has some credibility based on large numbers of people who prove it true. We must keep in mind there are exceptions to every personality rule.

Baby or Youngest

Now let's take a look at the Baby. We'll call Jason's and Emily's baby brother Andrew and look at life the way he sees it.

When he drops a rattle from his crib, odds are pretty good somebody will get it for him rather quickly. There are enough people in the house now that he need wail only a minute or two before someone comes to the rescue. By the time he's a toddler, the older kids are able to dress themselves and comb their own hair. But little Andy will get special treatment from both parents and even both siblings. That may still be the case when Andy is in school. For example, the family rushes around getting ready for church and is ready to go except Andy's sneaker is missing. Everyone rushes to aid in the search, as Andy sits and watches the activity with pleased fascination. He knows *he* can't find it. He's also learned this family of "grownups" can do anything, so why should he bother?

People make decisions for him, help him remember things, take responsibility for him and mention often he's "too little." Life can easily be a bowl of cherries for Andrew. *His motto is "I'm entitled."*

I fall into the youngest category myself. Deep down I like to think I'm entitled to whatever I want in life! I feel entitled to be slim, rich, gorgeous and ensconced in a magnificent castle designed to accommodate my love of comfort. Surrounded by my happy, adoring family, I should know no frustrations, have no problems to solve and be able to eat absolutely anything I want without gaining an ounce.

As you might imagine, with a secret wish like that, my life is a series of indignities! We youngests may think we're entitled, but the rest of the world doesn't know it.

I was fortunate to have as my counselor and colleague Dr. Maxine Ijams. She taught me about youngest children with a combination of love and humor. When I complained about the difficulty of having two people named Lee working in the same office, Maxine twinkled and said, "Of course! You're *entitled* to be the only Lee in the whole world!"

Another example of how youngest children feel they are entitled occurred when my youngest child, Lyle, and I went to eat at a cafeteria. You remove your food from the tray and set the empty trays on a nearby table for the waitress to clear. My husband Larry always takes my tray when I empty it. I sit comfortably while he finds a table on which to deposit it, along with his and the children's.

When Lyle and I went to the cafeteria by ourselves, both of us removed our dishes and held out our trays expectantly for the other to take. There was a second of confusion as we puzzled over why nothing was happening. Then we both laughed as we realized we were each "entitled" to that service.

A youngest child usually likes people a lot and expects them to like him. He's easy-going, social and skilled at getting people to do things for him. However, (there's always a con for every pro) he will also learn one sad truth—no one takes him very seriously. What does the baby know? He's just a baby, even though he's 50-years old.

I can vouch for that. When I was 50, I'd been trying for years to get my father to buy himself an exercise bike. I got absolutely no response. When Paul came to visit and suggested the same thing, my dad rushed right out and bought one. Clearly Paul was still the Smart One, and Leona was still the Baby.

Youngests can become spoiled princes or princesses who rule the house. Or they can become so defeated at feeling inadequate they may give up. Most of them land somewhere in between.

The youngest child develops skills at putting people in his service. He often becomes a charmer, able to convince anyone of anything and can become an excellent salesman, actor or con man. Youngests often annoy oldests, who are much more intent on being "proper" and "correct" than are their baby brothers or sisters.

Youngests are the easiest to identify. Dr. Ijams tells of a workshop she conducted on birth order. The group had only a few minutes left. The door opened, and a janitor walked in pushing his wastebasket, broom, bucket and mop. He was on his way across the auditorium to put his things in a closet when Maxine said, "Sir, would you mind waiting a few minutes until we're done?"

He shook his head and answered amiably, "No, I can wait." And he sat down comfortably in one of the chairs and looked around.

Maxine said, "Sir, can I ask you if you're the youngest child in your family?"

"I sure am. Why?" he asked.

"Because if you were an oldest child you would have opened the door and backed out quickly when you saw we were still in the room. If you'd been a middle you would have been very annoyed at us for being here when you needed to get into that closet. But as a youngest, you walked right in. It never occurred to you we would be anything but *delighted* to see you!"

Only Child

We must not overlook another special place in the family, the Only Child. Onlies seem to be a pretty good combination of firstborns and youngests. They have the same perfectionist tendencies as the oldests and are very responsible and reliable. Often they act like adults by the time they're 8. They may have some trouble relating to their peers while they're children because they are so frequently in the company of adults. But when they grow up, they've got it made. They're already proficient at being adults.

They never know the pain of dethronement. They continue feeling like the center of the universe. This has its pros and cons—the world doesn't know they're special and refuses to treat them that way. Nonetheless, the confidence they feel helps them achieve whatever they strive for. I think it's fascinating that most of our astronauts have been Onlies. Only children are often very bright. They feel special, so they qualify themselves for special positions. *An Only's motto is "I'm special."*

Onlies may not be as easy to live with as children who've had to learn sharing and cooperation with siblings. But the extra attention and encouragement they get from parents often balances things by promoting their self-esteem.

A Quick Glance at Your Birth Position

Let's examine the different birth positions. Consider your birth position, and see if you fit the mold.

Firstborns decide to "be good." They are proficient at pleasing their parents and others. They are responsible, reliable and dependable. A firstborn's motto is *"I was here first, and first I'll stay."*

The *second-born* child often acts as if he were in a race. He may be hyperactive and pushy. Though this behavior begins as he tries to gain importance and recognition in the family circle, it may become a lifetime decision. It accompanies him forever as he tries to achieve, accomplish, impress, surpass, often relentlessly driving himself without knowing why. A second-child's motto is *"I must try harder."*

A *middle-born* child often feels squeezed. He must cope with the rival he's competed with for his entire life who's still ahead of him. His life is further complicated by the baby. A middle child may feel unloved and abused. He may develop negative behavior to get attention. If it works, he may keep it, but if the payoff isn't there, he'll discard his behavior. He tries many ways to find his important spot. In the process, he develops worthwhile skills. A middle-child's motto is *"Life is unfair."*

The *youngest* child usually likes people and expects them to like him. He's easy-going and social. He develops skills at putting people in his service. He often becomes a charmer, able to convince anyone of anything. But people make decisions for him, help him remember things, take responsibility for him and mention often he's "too little." No one ever really takes him seriously. The youngest child's motto is *"I'm entitled."*

An *only child* is often a combination of firstborn and youngest. He has perfectionist tendencies and is responsible and reliable. He may have some trouble relating to his peers as a child. The world doesn't know he's special and refuses to treat him that way. But his confidence helps him achieve what he strives for. Only children are often very bright. They feel special, so they qualify themselves for special positions. An only child's motto is *"I'm special."*

Which Birth Position Is Best?

People often ask, "Which is the best position in which to be born?" My answer is, "All of them." None is best; none is worst. Each has its own set of advantages and disadvantages.

When I do workshops with a large group of people, I usually have a sampling of every birth-order position. Sometimes I ask the participants to divide into groups. "Firstborns over here, seconds there, middles here, youngests there and onlies over there." There is always a great deal of discussion as to what constitutes each definition. Inevitably there is some overlapping.

"There were 12 years between my brother and me. Does that make me a second?" is one typical question. The answer is no. More than 4 years between siblings starts the family constellation all over. The inquirer would be considered an Only with three parents because there were three people in her service and also three people telling her how to act.

"My sister and I are twins. What does that make me?" Twins invariably know who is older. They usually take on the characteristics of any other first and second children. They may love each other fiercely, but they may also be extremely competitive with each other. Both search intently for the special place that promises the most attention. So we determine which twin this is and he goes with the appropriate group.

"I'm a second child, but I'm also a middle. Which place do I belong in?" Though the second has the "I try harder" motto, he may qualify more for the middle child "life-is-unfair" belief system if he's the middle of three. That's because he had to cope with one above him and one below, a tough spot to be in. If he is the second of two, he will be a combination of "I try harder" and "I'm entitled."

Once people are in their assigned groups, they're given the task of discussing what it was like growing up in their homes, being the child in that particular birth position. I ask them to compile a list of factors they're aware of, common only to their position. It's interesting to watch the exercise take place and to see behavior that by now is quite predictable.

Someone in the firstborns usually asks (after raising a hand in the proper manner), "Do you want both pros and cons? Do you want them listed separately?" Firstborns like to know exactly what's expected of them before they begin. That's so they can "do it right!"

As the groups begin quietly discussing their origins, we begin to hear giggling and whoops of recognition from the youngests. And as they get increasingly noisier, the firstborns glare at them with obvious annoyance, but the youngests continue their behavior. Theirs seems to be more of a social gathering than a gathering of scientific evidence. Halfway through the allotted 15 minutes, a youngest may call out, "Does anybody have a pencil? Nobody here has one."

Immediately a firstborn will produce an extra pencil and even a sheet of paper for the ill-prepared youngests, trying to hide a feeling of superiority at being properly equipped. Of course youngests know *someone* will provide for their needs!

When time is called, the middles look shocked and protest en masse, "But we didn't have time to finish!" To middles, life is unfair. But they always turn in quite acceptable lists because middles have learned early to cope with distressing situations.

Firstborns always elect a spokesman who takes a neatly written list from the appointed secretary. He reads it easily and well because he's allowed sufficient time to look it over before standing up. Their organization is second to none and more than a little annoying to youngests, who are still whispering and giggling among themselves. Some memories common to firstborns are:
1. We had to take care of our brothers and sisters.
2. We were expected to do things perfectly; the others weren't.
3. We were blamed if there was an argument and told, "You should know better at your age."
4. We had more chores to do than the others.

Seconds say things like:
1. We could never measure up to the oldest's behavior.
2. We were always compared and found lacking.
3. They got to go places and do things we couldn't

because we were too young.
4. We had to wear their hand-me-downs.

Middles might offer:
1. The older ones got special privileges because they were older. The younger ones got spoiled. We never got anything special at all.
2. We were unnoticed, squeezed and taken for granted compared to the ones on either side of us.
3. We got lost in the shuffle.

Youngests maintain:
1. Nobody took us seriously. They all played together and said we were babies and couldn't play.
2. We got *all* the hand-me-downs.
3. They were always bossing us around, treating us like second-class citizens.
4. We were overprotected.
5. Nobody realized we were capable.

Onlies say:
1. It was no fun to be the only child in the house.
2. We had no one on our level, nobody to understand how it felt to be a kid.
3. If we wanted to play, we had to go *find* friends. We always envied our friends who had brothers and sisters.

And so it goes. The behavior and feelings of each person in a particular birth position are remarkably like those of others in the same position. And it will always be so. But even though the birth position affects your behavior and feelings, ultimately what matters is what you decide about your life. There are happy oldests and sad oldests, positive middles and negative middles, successful youngests and failed youngests. All were challenged by many of the same conditions, and all made decisions of how best to cope with them.

Why does it matter? Because you can gain awareness and understanding if you know something about a person's birth position. You can understand your own beliefs and feelings better, as well as those of the people you live with, work with and interact with every day.

Chapter 3

Values Are Important In What You Do, Think & Feel

The Bible tells us to "judge not." But judge we do—probably several times an hour. If we were not blessed with the capacity to judge, life would be quite meaningless to us. From the restaurant review in the morning paper to letters to the editor to editorials, we see other people's judgments. And we judge the judgments.

"Where does she get off criticizing that movie? It was a *great* picture!"

"This reporter likes that cafe? I can't believe it. The food is terrible."

"We should have elected Udall for president. He'd have gotten this country in good shape."

We disagree with folks whose judgments differ from ours. On the other hand, we are usually attracted to those whose values resemble our own. That's how clubs are formed. Churches embrace people who share their particular moral values, and members of a congregation feel a sense of belonging. Sometimes we question our neigh-

31

bors' religious preferences or their political leanings. But if we're "nice" people, we generously give them the right to live as they see fit. "Live and let live," we shrug, while deep down we *know* our values are the only sensible ones.

What Are Values?

A *value* is the relative worth or importance of something. Values determine much of the way you choose to live your life. Values are wonderful springboards to understanding. You would understand (if not approve) why I do the things I do if you could get inside my head and read my list of *shoulds* and *shouldn'ts*. My behavior, opinions and feelings make perfect sense when viewed through *my* private logic. Yours do too. The problem is we rarely realize how each other's private logic came to be, so it's difficult to understand and accept each other.

You may not fully understand your own value system and the circumstances from which it emerged. Frequently you're unaware of what is of value to you and how you measure these qualities in others. The lifestyle questionnaire addresses that issue when it asks you to describe each person in your family the way you saw them when you were a child. The words you choose to describe them define your particular values. When you think about family members, your mind automatically goes along certain corridors that are important to *you*.

One person might measure people in terms of strength and weakness. He might describe Dad as "big, strong, capable" and Mom as "gentle, submissive, quiet." Sister might be "bossy, aggressive, mean," and brother "sweet, scared, sickly." Whether descriptions are positive or negative, they all measure strength and weakness.

Another person might notice physical characteristics. "Mom was pretty, thin and tall. Dad was big, handsome and smiley. Mindy was fat, sloppy and ugly. Mandy was petite, fragile and pale." This person measures people now by the standard of how they look.

Productivity and achievement are often common values among achievers. Words like "busy, hard worker, go-getter, winner, ambitious, active" indicate an achievement value. So do words like "lazy, laid-back, dull." Assessment of those qualities, whether positive or negative, proves their importance.

Those who want to love and be loved might rate people as "loving, kind, devoted, giving, protective, throughtful, nice, fun, warm, friendly, sweet." They might also use the words "selfish, removed, unkind, mean, unfriendly, loners."

Depending on further insights into your family's relationships, you begin to see how you apply a certain value to yourself. The person who measured everyone on a scale of strength and weakness may have chosen to be strong or weak, depending on how those characteristics worked for members of his family.

If Mom got her way by being sweet and helpless, weakness may have come to be viewed as an advantage. If Mom's non-assertive ways earned her abuse and disrespect, her children might decide weakness is dumb and ineffectual. They would strive for strength.

Each child makes the decision for himself, even though they all watched the family dynamics unfold in much the same way. They interpreted the payoff differently. One might choose to be strong; another might choose to be weak. They will spend a lot of time gauging people's strength and weakness, including their own.

Strength would be a consideration in choosing friends.

You can imagine a first grader coming home to describe his new friend. "I got to sit next to Scott. Scott's really neat. He does whatever he wants to do. He's not scared of *anybody.*" We don't know whether the describer is weak or strong, but he certainly values and admires strength.

This same child might have different standards for different sexes. He might get a crush on Annie because "she's real good and real quiet. She never gets in trouble. Annie never talks."

He might choose friends he appraises as opposite from him to complement his own behavior. A strong child might seek out weak friends so he could be the leader. Or he might prefer the company of other aggressive children and find the weak ones "dull and wimpy." Either way, strength is his measuring stick.

Other Measuring Sticks

Your measuring stick can be found in your descriptions of family members, even though the adjectives you choose are generally not as concise and similar as the examples I've given. They're more likely to be a variety of descriptions. But there are always threads of similar values throughout. Below is one example:

- ❧ Dad was loud, domineering, strict.
- ❧ Mom was loving, quiet, friendly.
- ❧ Sean was teasing, bossy, playful.
- ❧ Kathy was smart, annoying, funny.
- ❧ Brian was mischievous, cute, messy.

In this value system there is a thread of lightheartedness. Words like "friendly, teasing, playful, funny, mischievous and cute" show playfulness is important to the subject. But there is also a strength/weakness element, indicating a choice between loud, domineering, strict and bossy traits or quiet, friendly, loving ones. Probably most of the children in this family would be a combination of funny and bossy, using lightheartedness along with determination to get their needs met.

The rest of this chapter is devoted to discussing particular parts of the lifestyle questionnaire and how your answers might be interpreted.

1. Names of parents and siblings.
Describe each person.

Like everything else in the lifestyle questionnaire, each interpretation must be evaluated within the context of the whole. The descriptive adjectives serve as a *starting point* in deciphering values. Later I demonstrate the technique by following a few lifestyles all the way through. These begin on page 135.

Sometimes a person's description of the family shows a sense of self-importance. Someone who believes she should be the center of the universe might see family members as positive or negative in the following ways:

- Dad was the greatest, fun; I was his favorite.

- Mom was nice, my confidante, my pal.

- Mike was wonderful to me, funny, helpful.

- Andrea indulged me, spoiled me, entertained me.

- George was mean, scared me; I didn't like him at all.

- I was pretty, special, spoiled.

It's no wonder this woman still feels like the Princess. That's how her family treated her (except for George, who is still in her disfavor for his shabby treatment).

It's interesting how "special" people usually can't resist making their descriptions longer than one adjective. It's as though they feel entitled to describe people as fully as they choose, no matter how lengthy the phrases.

- Dad was loving, good attention in the beginning but that stopped, distant.
- Mom drank a lot, never picked me up, never talked to me.
- Mark didn't want me around, overbearing, not close to me.
- I was shy, lonely, very confused.
- Tim was closer to me, my playmate; he loved me.

People in this subject's life are judged worthwhile or not in direct proportion to how much attention they give her.

You can see the adjectives in your family description serve two purposes. They clarify your family's values and reveal your own values as well.

I always tell clients I won't judge anyone they describe because I really can't take their word the people were like they sound. I'm hearing only *one person's* perception. But individual perception is the key to a lifestyle, and life is what we perceive it to be.

Occasionally I'll do lifestyle questionnaires with two or three members of the same family. It's amazing how differently they view each other. One woman described her father as gentle, kind and always there. Her sister said he was uncaring, selfish and distant. Obviously the man treated his daughters differently, but we can't be sure *how* differently.

It could be one daughter was very independent and didn't want a very close relationship with her father. For her, the amount of time they spent together was enough. Maybe the other daughter always hungered for more closeness with him and never felt fulfilled. To know what the father was really like, we'd have to get to know *him*. But because life is what we perceive it to be, the lifestyle technique is based only on *individual perception and interpretation*. That's the secret of its effectiveness.

2. Which family member was most like you?

This question continues the appraisal of yourself and others. It makes you dig for insights you may not have been aware of before.

- Mom was most like me because we're both strong and stubborn.

- Amy. She's also shy and creative like I am.

- I'm just like my dad. We're both good athletes.

The answers serve to point out more characteristics, good and bad.

3. Which family member was most different?

The question about who was most different does the same thing.

- Steven was different. He was always able to say what was on his mind. (Interpretation: I could never say what I was feeling.)

- Shanna was the smart one. (I felt like the dumb one.)

These self-images are often far from the truth. Studies show siblings in a family generally have similar IQ's, but they apply themselves to life in different ways. We've all heard stories about Albert Einstein flunking math, and I have no reason to doubt them. We're proficient in the areas in which we're interested. We become more proficient as we get encouragement for achievements in them. We tend to back away from subjects or areas of interest in which we seem to have no expertise. We spend our energies on activities we enjoy.

That just makes good sense. It has nothing to do with actual measurement of intelligence. Yet most of us quickly identify the sibling among us who was "the smart one," usually because of his or her good grades. Grades are only *one way* of measuring "smartness."

Nevertheless, we're not investigating the objective facts yet. We're investigating self-image. We're trying to establish *how* you see yourself. Later we analyze the validity of those beliefs.

4. As a small child, how did you get your way?

This question usually shows how you try to get your needs met *today*. Whatever worked for you then is something you keep in your bag of tricks to help you accomplish your goals for the rest of your life.

"I had temper tantrums," almost always means, "I still have temper tantrums." But today they may take a different form. A child who yelled and screamed at not getting his way may still yell and scream. Or he may resort to the silent temper tantrum of depression. Whatever the variation, it's safe to say he probably "loses" his temper to get his needs or wants met.

One young woman with a lot of charisma answered she got her way "by being extremely adorable!" She giggled and looked charmingly at her husband, who looked away with some hostility. Clearly she still practiced being extremely adorable. But the old tried-and-true method was no longer effective, at least not with her husband.

Many of us got good results by pleasing. Pleasers often

try that method first most of the time.

One man admitted to "being sick a lot and using it to my advantage." His honesty was refreshing. We all know people who seem to resort to sickness to get their needs met.

Sometimes people say, "I just *asked* for what I wanted, and I got it." They generally have difficulty when the real world doesn't treat them with so much kindness.

Another common response is, "I never got my way." I'm not sure whether that's really the case or whether it just seemed that way. But either way, that statement usually comes from people who are very discouraged and having a lot of difficulty getting their needs met now. They never developed the skill of assertiveness, whether it was their own fault or the fault of overly strict or overly pampering parents.

Some people have multiple ways of filling their needs. One lady told me, "I was charming. If that didn't work, I threw temper tantrums, then I pouted. I guess I was relentless. I kept trying different methods until something worked!"

It isn't surprising this woman is the president of a successful corporation. In case you're wondering why she sought counseling, she didn't. Her quiet, long-suffering husband did.

By now you're probably pretty clear on how *you* went about getting your needs met as a child. Perhaps you used some of the same methods other people did. Or you might have had some methods I haven't mentioned. I can almost promise whatever worked best is still your favorite method now. You probably use it whenever it is necessary.

If it isn't working, you may want to change it. When you stop and think about it, there are so many alternatives! The problem most of us face is we don't think about it. We don't change our approach; we keep our old favorite technique and try it harder and harder.

An angry temper-loser will get angrier and yell louder if he doesn't get his way. He might be very successful if he tried being kind and compassionate.

A pleaser may try harder to please. But he finds himself a doormat getting nothing but disrespect for all his hard work. The sullen pouter never gets his problems solved because he doesn't initiate the conversation necessary to achieve a solution. Instead he simply pouts longer and more intensely.

The people who never did get their way still don't.

So who does, and how do they do it? *Communicators* get their needs met. They determine they can risk disapproval, if need be, but they're going to say what's going on inside their heads and say it with respect.

We need to talk together endlessly and be willing to compromise, negotiate and keep trying to understand another person's position. People who do this are successful at getting their needs met and at enjoying many friendships and close relationships, all based on mutual respect.

5. What kinds of compliments did you receive?

Whatever compliments you received, chances are excellent you are very much a composite of them today.

"I was pretty, quiet, nice and never did anything wrong," one woman said. I'll bet you can guess what she's like. She's a joy to be around. But she's paying a very high price to maintain her image. She's such a pleaser she's not enjoying life much at all.

The beautiful, exhibitionistic "princess" quoted everyone as saying simply, "Pretty, pretty, pretty!"

Achievers were told they were "conscientious, hard-working, reliable and responsible."

The homemaker with the perfect house was told she was "very nice and neat, took good care of my things and could even make mud pies without getting dirty."

I'll bet comedians we laugh at on TV got lots of praise for their senses of humor when they were only in grade school. When fellow first graders roared at little Jimmy's antics, they were inadvertently planting seeds of future wit. By fifth grade, Jimmy was the much-admired class clown. By high school he was always the master of ceremonies at school assemblies. He may have had some leaning toward humor when he was only a tot. But the encouragement he received helped make it his claim to fame. What do you want to bet he'll be wowing them in the nursing home when he's 90?

It's a sure bet the artists you know were complimented on their artistic skills when they were little, as were the musicians. Athletes got admiration that fed their desire to improve, as did the mini-mechanics who "could fix anything."

As you look over your list of childhood compliments, I'll bet you're not surprised at how many of those traits are still a big part of your life. We can only wonder how many more skills we'd have today if our parents and teachers had noticed more of our early efforts with admiration.

6. What kind of criticism did you receive?

It's logical that attention and compliments help us make some behavior a permanent part of our lives. What isn't so logical is that we often become fixed in the *criticism* we received as children. This question about what kind of criticism you received as a child frequently uncovers characteristics you still have today.

Typical of some common responses are, "I always heard how I procrastinated. I never did my homework on time. I put off doing my chores as long as I could. I never finished anything."

At one time I would have thought a child who was told these things long enough and hard enough would eventually shape up and become more organized. Not so, I now believe. In fact, I'm almost sure that child is now an adult who procrastinates, puts things off and never finishes them.

It seems as though we took *all* the labels people gave us when we were small and used them to define how we would turn out someday. One woman who spoke very loudly all the time answered the question by saying, "They always told me I was too loud." Another client who looks perpetually grim says his father was forever criticizing him for not smiling. The plump gentleman admits he was always told he ate too much. We so easily become what we're told we are.

A charming 50-year-old lady sat down in my office one day and said, uncomfortably, "I have a personality disorder." Of course I was curious. When I asked her to tell me about it, she couldn't.

"I don't really know what it is," she explained. "I know only I have something wrong with me."

"*How* do you know?" I persisted.

"When I was in second grade," she explained, "my teacher stopped at my desk one day and looked at the paper I was writing. She criticized the way I made my T's and said loudly for all the class to hear, 'This child has a personality disorder.'

"Ever since then, I've known there was something wrong with me. But I don't know what it is. I've never told anyone before."

My heart went out to this lovely lady. She was as normal as you and I, but she'd spent years believing she was flawed because of some teacher's unthinking remark. We can only wonder what the teacher's "personality disorder" was to enable her to say something so without substance. Perhaps she had just read an article on handwriting analysis and was experimenting with her new-found "knowledge."

The few sessions I had with the woman bore out my conviction she was perfectly fine. I told her she could spend her next 50 years enjoying a new, healthy self-image.

Isn't it scary how vulnerable we are? It's amazing we're able to cope at all when we consider the pummeling our little psyches sustained during our childhoods. But the positive side is our ability to change the way we see ourselves at any time. Change is relatively easy once we have sufficient motivation. It's even easier when we gain some understanding of "how we got that way in the first place." All the questions we're pursuing help us identify our present attitudes and beliefs by understanding their origins.

7. Family mottoes

Another question concerns family mottoes. Usually there are more than just one or two. What were the most important values in your home when you were a child? In a few minutes you can usually arrive at a motto Mom might have had, whether or not she ever actually put it into a statement. You *knew* what she thought. You *knew* what kind of behavior she encouraged and what kind of thinking she discouraged.

Most mothers are excellent communicators verbally and non-verbally. We leave no stone unturned in trying to get our children to think like we do.

You might have taken Mom's motto to heart and made it your own, or maybe you rejected it. But I'll bet you know what Mom would have *wanted* you to believe in. Here are some examples:

- Don't make waves.
- Eat everything on your plate.
- You should never bother anyone.
- Be a good mother.
- Keep your nose clean.
- Take care of each other.
- Be quiet.
- We're special.
- Do your homework.
- Stay out of trouble.
- Love is what makes the world go round.
- Cleanliness is next to Godliness.

The question about mottoes also gives us insight into Dad's imprint on us. Occasionally both parents have the same motto. But generally they differ. Some common father values are these:

- Work hard.
- Money is everything.
- Do it right.
- You can be whatever you want.
- Don't make mistakes.
- Put others first.

- Get a good education.
- Enjoy life.
- Our family is right; others are wrong.
- Keep your nose to the grindstone.
- You can always do better.

Once you come up with your parents' mottoes, you have more food for thought about your decisions. Many times we become the product of parents' value systems. But just as frequently we deliberately reject one or the other.

For example, Mom harped on doing your homework and Dad pushed getting a good education. Together they made schoolwork a pain. You might have decided come hell or high water you were going to flunk, even if you might have preferred passing. Or you might have bought the package and ended up with a Ph.D. Either way, you decided to accept or reject the mottoes. It's helpful to get them down on paper just to see what you did with them.

One young couple having some marriage counseling were beside themselves trying to cope with each other's "wrong" attitudes. Sherry spent too much money, according to Marvin. She was not responsible, like a good wife should be. All she ever wanted to do was go out to dinner, go dancing, buy new clothes, throw parties.

Marvin, Sherry complained, was a stick in the mud who did nothing but read books on investments. His work as a stockbroker was the most important thing in life to him. He acted like they were poor, starving people. "He's a workaholic, and he's dull as dirt," she wailed.

All three of us laughed when they realized what their family mottoes would have been when they were children. Marvin's was, "Life is tough. Work hard, and save your money." Sherry's was, "Life is a banquet. Enjoy it to the hilt!"

Of course, family mottoes are often never articulated. They're simply there. One of the most common ways they're taught is by modeling.

In a home where one or both parents are pleasers, their behavior is usually very kind and considerate with outsiders. A child might be keenly aware of hostile silence between his parents all evening. Even a toddler is good at discerning bad feelings between his parents just by their body language. But suppose the phone rings midevening. Mom answers it with a cheery, "Hello" and immediately her behavior is transformed. Her face is alive, her voice has warmth and enthusiasm. She laughs easily and frequently throughout the conversation.

After 10 minutes, she hangs up. "Who was it, Mommy?" asks the child.

"Oh, it was Kim's teacher asking me to be a room mother. As if I had nothing else to do," Mom scoffs. "I wish some of those lazy mothers who do nothing would get off their sofas and help out once in awhile. Why is it I'm always the one everybody asks for help?" Her voice is angry.

"It's your own damn fault," says Dad, turning up the TV volume. "You try to look like Wonder Woman, and we get fast food junk for dinner." *His* voice is angry.

Then the doorbell rings. The neighbor wants to borrow the jumper cables. The child watches with fascination as Dad becomes the gentle, affable Good Guy, hurrying for the cables, offering to help. He seems happy to be able to care for his fellow man.

The child has just witnessed lesson #789 that teaches the family motto, "We must be nice to everyone outside the family."

Some of our values come through family teachings. Others we acquire on our own. The projective questions in the following chapter reveal other values that are important to you.

Chapter 4

Projecting Helps You Make Decisions

I used to think I was a little "weird" in some of my innermost thoughts. I wouldn't have dared admit them for fear everyone would know I wasn't playing with a full deck. But as I began reading self-help books and taking classes in psychology, I discovered behavior I thought was "strange" was really pretty normal.

One thinking process I now know is normal is *projection.* You *project* something that is a part of your thinking onto another person, animal or inanimate object. Have you ever reached for a can of soup in the supermarket and found the label torn? Then you put it back on the shelf and took an unmarred can? So far so good. But then did you feel sorry for the can you rejected? Some little voice deep inside your head said, "It's terrible to be left on the shelf over and over while people take all the other cans instead."

If you have thoughts like that, you're normal. (If you haven't, you're still normal!) But some people might feel so guilty after imagining how the poor rejected can felt they would buy it after all, torn label and all. Then they might wonder how the unmarred can they almost bought felt, having been replaced after it thought it was being bought!

That particular stream of consciousness is focused on a soup can. It might sound laughable if you don't pursue that thought process. But chances are excellent you project some of your feelings onto something somewhere.

Picture a big dog running down an alley. He stops to sniff at garbage cans, occasionally tipping one over to eat the scraps he smells. One person seeing him might feel very sorry for the dog, thinking, "Poor thing probably doesn't belong to anyone. He has to go searching for food and probably feels hungry a lot of the time. What a dreadful life."

Another person might be thinking, "What a life! That lucky animal is free to go, see and do whatever he wants. He doesn't have to answer to anyone. He gets fresh air and exercise and probably more food than he can eat."

No one really knows how the dog feels about the whole thing. But you project your thoughts and attitudes onto the dog.

People with many fears believe everyone is in danger. Lonely people see loneliness in every face. The sight of a man sitting on a park bench might conjure up the thought, "That poor miserable guy has no job, no home and no family."

Someone else might project, "I'll bet he loves sitting there in the sun, enjoying his relaxation. I wish I could do that."

Projection is a process you can't avoid, even if you tried. You project constantly about many different things. It helps you decide what you're going to do with your life.

Projecting how animals must feel when caught in a trap drives some people into joining animal-rights coalitions. Projecting how a person must feel being killed can lead people to a "Right to Life" movement. Projecting how a pregnant, unwed teenager must feel can lead someone else to work for laws allowing abortion. Projection is a useful technique in helping you understand another person's viewpoint and gaining more insight into your own.

An interesting exercise in projection is to ask people in a group to choose any object or part of the room they would like to be. Answers tell quite a bit about each person's attitude or mood at that moment.

"I'd like to be the big beam that holds up the ceiling. The whole building would collapse if that weren't there."

"I'd like to be that beautiful plant. Someone would water me and feed me."

"I'd be the stained-glass window. It seems to dominate the room; everyone stares at it. It's magnificent."

"I'd be one of the books on the shelf. No one would really notice me, yet I'd get to be here and know what's going on."

"I'd be the door. Everyone would have to go through *me* to go in or out of the room."

All these projections were offered at a church seminar I attended recently. You can guess which person was the "important" one who felt responsible for everything and carried the weight of the world on his shoulders. You also can recognize the passive woman who depends on others to take care of her. Can you see the striking exhibitionist who craves attention, the unobtrusive man who prefers to be left alone and the person who likes to be in charge and run things?

Projecting Stories

Projection is a simple technique, but it's very revealing. Some questions on the lifestyle questionnaire illustrate how we project our wishes and attitudes onto story characters, animals and other fantasies.

With women, the all-time favorite story is *Cinderella*. They usually like the feeling of romance and specialness and the idealistic way the good, sweet person wins over the evil people. Cinderella was patient, long-suffering, unappreciated, hardworking and beautiful. Many women see themselves as being very much like her.

There are always variations, however, in people's reasons for choosing that story. Fourteen-year-old rebellious Sara said she liked it "because Cinderella got what she wanted!" We can guess Sara intends to get what she wants a good part of the time, regardless of the barriers she must overcome.

Men often choose stories with adventure in them, like *The Hardy Boys, Tom Sawyer* or *Swiss Family Robinson*. They usually identify with the hero. What do they like about these stories? "He had so much freedom and got to do so many exciting things." "He met impossible demands fearlessly and emerged victorious."

People almost always identify with the hero or heroine of a story, but occasionally I get a surprise. One client's favorite fairy tale was *Snow White*. I expected the lovely lady to have identified with Snow White, but she chose Dopey. "I always felt like I was the dopey one in the family," she said.

A favorite of both sexes is *The Little Engine That Could*, especially among firstborns who are into perfectionism, achieving and always being first. The ideal of finally overcoming great odds and winning the challenge usually keeps their noses to the grindstone.

One woman remembered Jo in *Little Women*. "She marched to a different drummer, and she took risks. She was strong, had courage and really was everybody's favorite." Another person might have chosen Beth as "everybody's favorite" because "she was so sweet, good and never caused trouble." We admire others for the traits we'd like to see in ourselves.

Projecting as an Animal

The question, "If you had to come back in another life as an animal what would you be, and why?" also helps you project your feelings. When you project as an animal, your answer is a description of how you wish we were treated.

Frequent choices are a puppy or a kitten "because they're so cute and cuddly, and everyone loves them." People who would choose to be these animals are looking for cuddling, loving and pampering.

A couple who was seeing me for marriage counseling both chose dogs, but for different reasons. His reason was, "Dogs get lots of love. People take care of them, feed them and pet them. They have no problems or responsibility."

The wife, on the other hand, explained, "Dogs are man's best friends. They're loyal and loving to their masters no matter what. A dog will always be there to cheer you up. He'd even give his life for you."

Both partners were different kinds of "dogs." The husband wanted to be cared for, loved, fed and petted. The wife was willing to love, be true, cheerful and loyal. Actually their relationship was very good because each had expectations that blended well with the other's.

Another popular choice is a bird, for the freedom it has. Being able to go wherever you want is a plus. Another is "being able to look down on everyone." That desire usually indicates a quest for superiority.

Now and then I hear surprising choices. One of my favorites came from Valerie, a young woman who saw her propensity for complicating her life. "I'd be a tarsier," she said, with a wry smile. "They're a kind of monkey who pees in their own nests." Valerie's greatest strengths are her delightful sense of humor and her willingness to admit *she* is responsible for most of the problems in her life.

My choice? I'd be a lion. They're beautiful, strong and get to do pretty much what they want!

Projecting a Remembrance

Another projection question asks what you'd like your tombstone to say about you. The answers generally fall into two categories: rich-famous-successful or loving. A few people incorporate both, but most hit one image or the other. Some typical descriptions are:

- He was a hard worker.
- Cared more about others than he did himself.
- Devoted mother and wife.
- She knew how to enjoy life.
- Brought joy to everyone.
- His sense of humor was the best.
- Thought only of his family.
- She fought for what she wanted.

An entertaining variation on the rich-and-famous theme was one pretty young woman's response. A bit of an exhibitionist, she was beautifully dressed, perfectly coiffed and heavily made up. She rested her chin on her bejeweled and finely manicured hand and said eagerly, "I know. I'd like a portrait of *me* on the stone! And lit up in neon at night!"

Projecting Others Talking About You

The imagining mind is responsible for much of life, and projection is a product of the imagination. Imagination is a great tool for uncovering attitudes you may not know you hold. The fantasy in which you imagine hiding and overhearing people talk about you demonstrates this point.

When I did this exercise, I imagined I was playing in a large, lighted closet that had become *my* area. I kept all my toys there and would sit in it for hours playing paper dolls or "school teacher."

I imagined my mother saying, "Leona is a good girl."

Dad agreed, "Yes, she is."

My response was, "I'm really not that good. But I mustn't let them know it, or maybe they won't love me."

My one-word feeling was "uncomfortable" because I was aware of the danger of losing their approval.

The important part of this exercise is your *response*. It doesn't matter what the fantasized people say. What matters is how you respond to their statement.

My response shows a lack of self-esteem. Had my self-esteem been better, I might have thought to myself, "Isn't it nice I'm so good. I'm glad they see it and appreciate it!"

If I had pictured two friends, I might have imagined them saying, "Leona is fun to be with. Let's find her and see if she wants to play."

But low self-esteem would cause me to respond with

the thought, "Gee, I'm glad they want to play with me. I'd better not do anything to make them mad at me."

Responses are predictably consistent with a person's degree of self-esteem. Those who like themselves declare that fact, regardless of the direction of conversation. They don't buy negative criticism from fantasized people if their self-image is positive.

Suppose I imagined someone saying, "Leona is spoiled and selfish," and someone answering, "She sure is; I hate her."

If my self-esteem is high, I might respond, "I'm not spoiled or selfish; they are!" Or "Those liars. I know I'm really wonderful." But if my self-esteem is low, my thoughts would be very different. "How horrible they know I'm no good." Or "I'd better not let people get to know me; they won't like me."

The saddest factor in poor self-esteem is our unwillingness to believe the good things we're told. If we're down on ourselves, we continue to reject words of praise unless we decide that we're becoming worthy. We often fiercely agree with negative comments about ourselves because they prove what we've "known" all along—we're not good enough.

I believe most people lack a strong sense of self-worth. As babies, we have no self-esteem. In fact, we're born feeling inferior. We spend our lives trying to achieve some sense of self-worth. If your answers show you to be low in that area, join the club. It's reassuring to me to know I'm normal when I see evidence of my poor self-image. Rare is the person who seems to have had strong self-esteem all his life. Most of us gain a little every year.

The other attitude measured by the "hiding and overhearing" fantasy is how you have decided you can best fit into the world in which you know live.

For me, the statement, "I mustn't let them know I'm not that good, or maybe they won't love me" demonstrates one of my early decisions. I wanted to avoid the possible discomfort of anyone's disapproval. I put on a happy face, was a perpetual Kewpie doll, didn't make waves, didn't show anger. I wasn't real. That decision about how I could best fit into the world is evident from my response.

Chances are your response to your imaginary overheard conversation will reveal one of your early decisions about how to fit in with the world. This makes the "hiding" exercise an excellent tool for better understanding yourself.

Chapter 5

You Can Clarify Your Problems

Sometimes people come into my office to get counseling for a specific problem, like adjusting to a divorce or dealing with a rebellious teenager. At other times, a person will come in for a mental-health "tune-up" because he wants to learn to feel more positive about himself. Sometimes people aren't quite sure what they want from counseling. They just know they aren't as happy as they'd like to be.

That's where the next questions on the lifestyle questionnaire come in handy. They let you decide what you would have liked to change about your childhood. It's fun to have a magic wand at your disposal, if only in fantasy. It's interesting to look back at your early days and pick out what you'd like to have been different.

Changing the Past with a Magic Wand

Some people say if they had a magic wand, they would

change the behavior of other family members.

"My father would have been more compassionate, less restrictive and more loving to me."

"I wish I'd had brothers and sisters."

"I wish my big sister had gone to live with somebody else."

"Mom wouldn't have been so scared of everything and overprotective."

"My brother would have been closer to my own age so I'd have had help in learning to get along with people."

"Dad (or sister Rose or brother Ted) wouldn't have died."

"I wish my parents had been more caring and loving and helped me grow up to be a more responsible adult."

You can probably find circumstances that explain some personality trait or behavior flaw you have that you don't want. It's good to look back and see how events of the past inspired you to make decisions you still live with. But you can't allow yourself to be stuck in patterns you now see as negative or destructive.

If parents had helped instill responsibility, everyone would have grown up responsible. But you can decide to become responsible at *any time* in your life. You'll enjoy a sense of power when you give yourself permission to go beyond the restrictions your parents mistakenly put on you.

Most of us have some regrets about our early training. But most of us can admit our parents were trying to do a good job. They made some mistakes that affected our lives adversely, perhaps for many years. But now we're grown up; we can and should correct any errors that continue to trouble us in ourselves.

Sometimes a person doesn't want to grow up or change. Instead he continues to blame his parents. For example, if he doesn't want to make the effort to become socially comfortable, he might prefer repeating, "My family never did anything social, so I never learned how to be comfortable in social situations." But once he sees it as a cop-out, he can learn how. All it takes is the decision he *wants* to change and the courage to begin.

Finding magic-wand changes in childhood gives you more insight into the origins of today's problems and hang-ups. Increased understanding allows you to be kinder to yourself in recognizing how your flaws began. Don't chastise yourself for having made faulty decisions when you were little. You did the best you could. But you can revel in your power to change.

Changing the Present with a Magic Wand

With that same magic wand, would you change anything about your life right now? What would it be?

"My drinking."

"I'd be more tolerant of other people and not have such high expectations."

"I'd take more risks."

"I'd quit hiding from the world."

"I'd have a better job, one with some potential."

"I would have a family of my own."

"I wouldn't be so timid about speaking up for what I want."

Whatever your particular magic-wand wizardry would produce can be produced in reality. *You* can make it happen! You don't even need a magic wand.

If you're drinking too much, go to an AA meeting. Get some counseling. Have the courage to do the thing you fear to do.

You want a family? Find a mate. If you wanted a pair of

shoes, you'd go to a shoe store, wouldn't you? If you want a spouse, you have to go where there are spouses-to-be. Prospective mates can be found in churches, exercise clubs, work places, schools, bars, classes, interest group clubs and friends' houses. They're practically never found in your own living room, where you sit and sigh heavily about your parents' bad influence.

The only way to find a better job is to start looking. Find out what the qualifications are. Begin the process of education and/or experience that's going to make you valuable in that job.

We All Take Risks

Reluctant to risk? Everyone is! But we all take some kind of risks more easily than other kinds. My daughters, Laurie and Lisa, told me one day they'd come up with four basic types of risks that they think encompass all risks. I think they're right; see what you think. They list risks as physical, financial, social and emotional.

Physical risks are anything potentially dangerous to your body. Driving motorcycles, hang-gliding, doing drugs, engaging in sports, racing cars and mountain climbing are physical risks.

Financial risks include dabbling in stocks and bonds, buying and selling real estate, going into business. These risk-takers do anything where losing money is a distinct possibility. But so is making money.

Social risks are performed in a social setting where disapproval is not a surprise. Dressing in conspicuous, avant-garde clothes for a conservative business meeting qualifies as a social risk. So is talking up the Democratic party in a room full of Republicans. Speaking out for a new cross-town freeway at a city-council meeting where most people are opposed is a social risk. It's saying what you think and feel, even though it may be unpopular.

Emotional risks include sharing feelings, baring your soul and falling in love easily. People who take emotional risks have no qualms about forming wonderful new relationships, even though they've been hurt by past relationships. They're open and honest in conversations and feel happy when they're able to deepen friendships.

Just for fun, rate these four categories from easiest to hardest for you. It's comforting to see everyone takes some risks. Nobody is a total scaredy-cat. But we still tend to avoid areas in which risking is difficult.

If you want to wave your magic wand and take more risks, find some in the categories that are hard for you. You'd grow by leaps and bounds if you started focusing on those areas. The only way you can grow is by deliberately doing the things you fear to do. That's what risking is all about.

For me, the challenge would be physical risks. I cannot imagine rafting down the Colorado River. The very phrase "camping out" gives me hives. If I practice what I preach, I'll commit myself to stretching in that direction.

What problem or problems did you have in your childhood that you still have now? Occasionally someone doesn't have any. Some people have managed to lick all the problems they dealt with as a child. They're the exceptions to the rule. Most people still struggle. Often you can see huge, sweeping problems that are as disconcerting now as they were 20, 30 or 40 years ago, like Arlene's.

The Problem with Expectations

"I still have expectations that don't get met," Arlene said. She speaks for many of us. Actually that one "fault" may encompass dozens of miniproblems that plague us in our relationships today. We expect our spouses to know what will make us happy and act accordingly. We expect our children to take on the same values and beliefs we teach them.

We expect life to be fair. We expect employers to notice our hard work and reward us financially or verbally. We expect our parents to let us live our own lives and not keep telling us what to do. We expect courtesy from store clerks. We expect the exterminator to kill our bugs. Unfortunately, we're *constantly* disappointed!

We should have learned to let those expectations go because they cause us so much grief. But many of us have a hard time doing that.

The more expectations we have, the more we're hurt. I admire people I know who seem able to roll with the punches and enjoy most of what life deals them. I'm the first to admit I'm not one of them.

My husband often is. One of my problems with vacationing is the disappointment I usually encounter because of my expectations of just "how things will be." Getting ready for a trip to San Diego last summer included forming expectations. Planning what to pack, I pictured the entire family, happy and serene, eating at Anthony's, enjoying the harbor cruise and eagerly shopping at Seaport Village.

I didn't expect the flat tire outside Yuma. I didn't expect the motel to be in the flight pattern, so I didn't anticipate planes roaring over us every 4 minutes all night long. And when we changed motels the next day, I didn't expect the neighbors to have a dog that barked all night. Having to wait 45 minutes to be seated at Anthony's was not part of my plan. I didn't know the wind would be so chilly on the harbor cruise or the boys would be unimpressed with Seaport Village and would sit looking morose. Nothing was how I'd pictured it. You get the idea.

On the other hand, I look in amazement at Larry, who looks happier than ever when we're on vacation. He doesn't seem to have any expectations. While we stand in line at Anthony's, he points out sea gulls and boats and tells jokes. He sleeps through the airplanes and the dog. If he doesn't feel like shopping, he whips out a book and reads contentedly until we're done. I both admire and loathe him.

Like Arlene, I'm trying to lower my expectations. This year, I'm determined to go to San Diego without a single picture in my mind and be open to whatever happens. If I keep trying every year, I may enjoy vacations by the time I'm 100-years old!

Other Childhood Problems

Many people have more specific answers to the question about what childhood problems they still have. Cyndy said, "Accepting compliments. I'm embarrassed being complimented, yet I long for them."

That's easier to deal with. It's mostly a matter of practice. Admittedly, we can't practice all the time because most of us don't get that many compliments. But when we do, we must make ourselves say a warm, "Thank you!" then shut our mouths. The temptation is to dispute the compliment, explain why it isn't true or give someone else the credit. That's because we're embarrassed.

Cheryl regrets she still wants to be the best at everything. But she still feels only mediocre. That "need" to be best is often caused by parents who keep pushing perfectionism and competition in their desire to help us improve ourselves. Even if they don't push us, they may model it themselves, which teaches it just as effectively.

I was always grateful my parents never made a big deal of good grades. They said they expected average work from us, and that was fine with them. However, both Paul and I always got good grades because it was more fun than getting bad grades. We both grew up achievers and drive ourselves fairly relentlessly.

As I look back, I remember my mother telling us how proud she was of her work as a telephone operator. She placed calls faster than anyone else and was promoted to supervisor. As she described her jobs when she was young, they all showed "superior performance" in the way she worked.

My father's voice had the same pride in his work as he recounted stories of taking shorthand faster than the other clerks. He worked for the Santa Fe Railroad and was chosen to take investigations because his reporting was without error.

Although my parents didn't push us to excel in school, the message was "Excel! It feels great."

The negative side is the tendency to put yourself down when you don't excel, like Cheryl does. Doing a mediocre job is perfectly appropriate in many of the things you do. It's all right to clean the sink imperfectly sometimes. But if you bought the message in childhood you need to be the best at everything, you might want to consciously change that decision now.

Another common lifetime problem is "seeking approval." Many people did it as children and are still doing it. Pleasers have an inordinate need (actually it's a *desire*) to please and/or to avoid disapproval. It's so common it's explored in depth beginning on page 135. If you still seek approval, your belief and resulting action might be any of the following.

"Seeking everyone's approval."

"My fear of upsetting anyone."

"My need to please."

Any of these answers reveal you as a pleaser.

My friend Michele defined her problem as "lying." It seems as a child she quite successfully got out of trouble by bending the truth. She became so good at it she got impressively creative. Although she's Jewish, one day when she was very young she went into a confessional in a Catholic church. She confessed to the priest she'd lied to her mother. As she tells it, the priest told her not to bother with such minor sins; it was a waste of his time. That reassured her lying was nothing to worry about, and she became even more skilled at it.

I got to know Michele when she came for marriage counseling; she shared with me her propensity for lying. Though I tried my best to convince her to stop, I had to be impressed with her creativity.

She did things like set up romantic scenes for her husband to find. If he went to a football game with the boys, Michele would be asleep by the time he got home. But he would discover two drained wine glasses on the coffee table in the living room, romantic records on the floor and cigarette butts in the ashtray. Michele didn't smoke, but she'd go out to the garbage can in the alley and find cigarette butts to lend credibility to a staged tête-à-tête that never happened. Her purpose was to make her husband jealous.

She delighted in her ability to give mistaken impressions and still does. The marriage ended in divorce. But Michele has many suitors, none of whom know about the others. For her, lying may be a problem, but she sees no real need to stop. Until she does, she'll continue doing it.

Clarifying or identifying problems doesn't mean you

have any intention of changing them or even that you *want* to change them. I may go to my grave hanging onto the very traits and beliefs that have caused most of the troubles I've encountered in my life. I have that right. But it's helpful to recognize them if only for the purpose of making a conscious decision of whether or not I want to keep them.

In the next section, we'll examine how childhood memories can help identify some of the beliefs you acquired early in life.

Chapter 6

Early Memories Affect Your Beliefs

What is your earliest recollection? Think back to your childhood, and get in touch with the earliest incident you can remember. Don't count general memories like, "Every vacation we went to my aunt's house." Look for a specific incident.

My earliest memory was having my Uncle Jerry spend Easter with us when I was four. I remember having an Easter basket full of jelly beans, a few eggs and one special prize—a chocolate bunny. Uncle Jerry came over and admired my basket. Then he reached in, took the chocolate bunny, unwrapped the cellophane and *ate my bunny!* I looked on in horrified disbelief but did absolutely nothing about it except remember the incident with great self-pity for the rest of my life. You might not be surprised to learn I never forgave Uncle Jerry. And I never liked him after that.

That's my earliest memory, so it's a pretty good indication of a lifestyle decision I had made before that dastardly deed took place. Even when I am a poor, helpless victim, I dare not make waves. I must tolerate disrespect and shut up about it but never forgive or forget! I saw myself as being helpless but good. I clung tenaciously to that self-image for a long time.

Another early memory was playing hide and seek with my family and some friends after supper on a warm summer evening when I was about 7. It was dusk, and I was pressed close to the house trying to avoid being discovered. I looked down and saw a black-widow spider a few inches from my ankle. In total panic I raced, wild-eyed, into the yard, shouting for help in the face of this grave danger. Predictably my family was there on the spot with concerned faces. I pointed out the offending spider. They all ran for shovels to kill it, while I shuddered at how close I'd been to tragedy!

At least that's how I remember it happening. That's what's important in this exercise. If I checked out the incident with my parents or my brother I'd possibly hear very different recollections of what happened. Actually I doubt my brother would remember it at all. But its importance in my mind points up the amazing value our early memories have.

Of the millions of incidents you experience, you discard the memories of most of them. The memories you keep are carefully chosen to teach you, warn you and guide you in your decision making for the rest of your life.

It's entirely possible the black widow was 15 inches from my ankle and only my father got a shovel or perhaps a broom. But my recollection serves to dramatize my situation of danger and helplessness and my position of importance in the family circle. Although I may have unconsciously embellished the details, that version tells a lot about how I saw myself and the world I lived in.

According to Alfred Adler, memories are "windows of the soul." They tell us so much about ourselves and how we see life. They are valuable tools for self-understanding because of the way they expose various aspects of our unique belief systems.

If the memories I've just recounted show a frail, helpless, quiet, oh-so-good child, the next ones demonstrate quite a different facet of my personality.

When I was about 5, my father invited an out-of-town friend home for dinner one night. The man was very nice to me, admiring my doll collection and the dress I wore. I was absolutely thrilled with some unexpected attention from a strange man! When we sat down to dinner, the grownups talked about things that didn't include me. I began to hunger for more attention. Finally I could stand it no longer, and I abruptly stood up on my chair.

Needless to say, all heads swung toward me. After a moment's puzzled silence someone said, "I think Leona wants to be noticed." Everyone laughed. Although I felt a wave of embarrassment, I enjoyed the attention immensely. Any discomfort I felt was worth it for the feeling of being "center stage" I got to enjoy.

To this day, my family kids me about how much I love being center stage. Anyone who saw me standing on my chair at age 5 might have predicted I'd be doing it forever, hopefully in more socially acceptable ways. Today I may seek center stage by giving a seminar for a church group or playing the piano for a sing-along. In my heart I'm still the little girl standing on the kitchen chair drinking in attention.

Anyone interpreting my memories might have guessed I see myself as a "princess" who loves being noticed, pampered and cared for. Certainly my father's early nickname for me, "Kewpie," helped me decide I must go through life smiling contentedly (like the doll I was nicknamed for), not making waves. I must enjoy being cute, cuddly and not too responsible. Others should take care of me.

Youngest children have the motto, "I'm entitled," so my next early memory fits very well. When I was about 8, my brother had an unusual pencil. It was yellow, with a plastic holder. Paul had replaced the eraser with a tiny cork. I thought it was marvelous and asked him if I could have it. He said "No." One day when he was in school I was home with a cold. I sneaked into his room and took the pencil from his cigar box of treasures. When he came home, I was brazenly sitting at the kitchen table, writing with it.

Of course he noticed it and said, "Hey, that's my pencil!"

To which I self-righteously replied, "It is *not*. It's mine. I have one exactly like yours."

Knowing I was lying, he chose to say nothing. He looked at me for a minute or two, then left the room.

Talk about guilt! He was my brother, whom I loved more than I could have expressed! I knew I shouldn't steal, so the whole thing went completely against my moral values. I stole, then I lied. How could I have been such a sinner? I didn't dare confess; I would have been too humiliated.

I decided it was a guilt I would have to live with, and I lived with it for 45 years. When Paul was visiting me a few years ago, I shared with him the years of guilt I'd endured for stealing his pencil. His puzzled reply was, "*What* pencil?" (Certainly that was a better lesson in morality than all the nuns' warnings of the wages of sin. I sinned, and I suffered!)

But looking back, I can see my youngest-child motto

was fulfilled in that memory. "I'm entitled." I simply *took* what I wanted. The fact it caused me so much guilty grief points out another aspect of my belief system, "I'm good and never do anything wrong."

Conflicting Beliefs and Values

Conflicting beliefs and values can be a double bind. This problem often shows up in early memories, as it does in real-life events every day. Both conflicting beliefs and values are valid parts of your mental makeup. The more clearly you see the beliefs you hold, the more easily you become their master. As you understand and accept your beliefs, you can confidently control them. You can let yourself decide which beliefs you're going to honor, instead of letting yourself be driven by them.

You know a belief like "I'm good and never do anything wrong" is ridiculous. No one is *that* good! But such a belief indicates a direction in which you strongly lean. All the beliefs you recognize from early memories are exaggerations of the truth. They're like caricatures drawn by artists. They play up traits to make a point or make a statement.

Recurring Themes or Patterns

If you write down a dozen of your early recollections, you'll probably find two or three recurring themes or patterns. For instance, in the four memories I've recounted, two portray me as a poor, helpless waif who depends on others to treat me well or badly. I am clearly a receiver of other people's actions. But the other two show me as a strong, determined child who will go after whatever she wants—a *doer* rather than a receiver.

Most people are made up of combinations of those two self-images. There is a third, the observer. An observer spends much of his life watching others and drawing conclusions about life in a passive way. Examples might be, "I remember swinging on my swing, watching my little sister make mud pies. After she got them all laid out and decorated with little stones, this big bully from next door came over and knocked them all off the table. I felt really sorry for her. I learned you can't trust people. They're out to get you."

Another observer memory might be, "My big brother came home late from a date. My father locked him out of the house. I was lying in bed listening to the two of them yell at each other and feeling scared. I never would have done anything wrong like that, to get my dad mad at me. He had so much power. (I must avoid getting in the way of powerful people.)"

Those recollections point out the early decisions this person made by observing then drawing conclusions. Many of our beliefs are formed in the same way.

Mistaken Beliefs

Habits that are difficult to break are frequently the result of mistaken beliefs. Let's look at some mistaken beliefs inspired by receiver memories and decisions.

If you see yourself as the helpless receiver of other people's actions, you're in a vulnerable position. Things are fine as long as people treat you kindly, but you're in bad trouble when they don't.

People with all receiver memories find it hard to accept the fact they're responsible for most of what happens to them. They decide at an early age that others are to blame for all their unhappiness. Only on rare occasions will they come upon "good" people who treat them as they like to be treated.

Receivers can also have happy memories. "I was sitting on my front step embroidering when I was just a little thing, maybe 4 or 5. A lady walked by, stopped and looked at my embroidery. She complimented me on my skill for such a little girl and gave me 2 pennies out of her purse. I was thrilled!"

In that memory, the subject was a doer as well as a receiver. But the main thrust of the recollection was the unexpected gift from a stranger. You're happier if you have receiver memories in which people were kindly benefactors rather than disrespectful abusers. But you're prone to disappointment when you measure your chances of happiness by how other people treat you.

The most well-adjusted people I know have a lot of doer memories. "I remember putting on a pair of my mother's high-heeled shoes one Sunday. I was just 6 or 7, and I walked all by myself to a church in the next block. I marched in proudly and sat in the front row. I felt so pleased and grown up!"

"My friend and I skipped school and used our lunch money to take a bus downtown. We had such a good time. But I remember how guilty I felt when I got home and Mom had no idea I'd been downtown instead of at school."

Doers often remember bad incidents as well as good ones. But doers see themselves as being responsible for their actions and their feelings. The big advantage is when you recognize your own power to live your life to make yourself happy or sad, you also recognize your freedom to make the choice.

Positive and Negative Recollections

In helping people gain self-understanding, I ask them for a variety of memories. Most of us seem to remember bad ones more easily, but that doesn't mean we're negative people filled with anger and fear. It means those incidents were so uncomfortable we must not allow that kind of thing to happen again. Unconsciously we've kept those memories to protect us.

All our negative recollections demonstrate "what I try to avoid in life." Positive ones demonstrate "how life should be."

Looking at examples of my own early memories, it seems I try to avoid being ignored or taken advantage of. For me, life should be getting noticed, being cared for, getting what I want and feeling important.

You need to recognize your wishes, unrealistic though they may be, and put them into a sensible perspective. The more understanding you have about your ideals and fears, the more easily you can be their master, rather than the other way around.

However, you can't use them to excuse bad behavior. That's copping out on responsibility. It would be ridiculous for me to demand special treatment with the rationale, "Even my early memories prove I should get my way and be center stage, so you have to cater to me." Being able to see myself resorting to those childlike feelings helps me chuckle at myself. It lets me switch to a more mature attitude—I can't have everything I want.

The old adage, "It's not wrong to get head lice, but it's wrong to keep them," applies here. Don't blame yourself for forming unrealistic expectations as a child. But if you choose to keep them once you know better, then you have only yourself to blame. A hard look at your memories helps you see your mistaken decisions. Then you can change them.

The Feeling of Belonging

No matter how different beliefs and expectations are, everyone shares a universal desire—to *belong*. Belonging, or feeling included, worthwhile and significant, takes different forms for everyone. You can identify your own unique goal of importance in your early memories.

Recently I got to know a young man named John; he was discouraged with his non-assertiveness. He felt his shyness and reticence kept him from interacting with people and prevented him from enjoying good relationships. John was perpetually disappointed in himself for his lack of courage and had very little self-respect. He had become so afraid of rejection he was almost immobile. He was becoming reclusive instead of reaching out for the one thing he wanted most in life—contact with other people.

John's memories began with his earliest one. "I was in my crib. Aunt Molly peeked into the room. She saw me trying to climb out of the crib. She talked me into lying down and going to sleep. I felt so much love, seeing her love for me."

My interpretation of John's recollection would be *though I might want to climb out of my crib, I should lie down and go to sleep. I mustn't be assertive and adventurous. If I lie quietly and passively, people will love me.*

With that decision made when he was just a baby, such behavior became a means to an end. It was John's way of gaining approval. Subsequent incidents lent credibility to his belief system and kept him going in the direction he was testing out.

Even his simplest recollection is significant. "One day during recess, my parents drove up to school. They talked to the teacher through the car window and drove off without talking to me. I felt so upset and disappointed, I cried."

Interpretation—*being ignored or left out by people upsets me very much. It's one thing I must try to avoid. I need their love.*

In another memory, John hoped not to play sports at school. He was afraid of not knowing what to do. He was afraid of doing poorly and being embarrassed.

Interpretation—*I mustn't take risks. I'll avoid situations in which I might do badly because it's too horrible to feel embarrassed.*

In three memories, you can see John's decision to stay safe, avoid risks, be passive and not "get out of the crib."

The following is a memory describing his view of how life *should* be. "On Saturday afternoon, I got to go into town with my best friend. We'd would sit on the step of the drugstore and watch people and talk and laugh. I felt so much pleasure doing that."

Interpretation—*I hunger for companionship. I would be so happy if I could enjoy the company of a best friend, watching people, talking and laughing. I want that!*

In yet another memory, John told me, "Teacher had a rule we had to go to the bathroom before or after recess. One day, I got caught going *during* recess. My punishment was being tied to the flagpole during 2 days' recess, so I couldn't play. I was so embarrassed."

Interpretation—*I must always be obedient. If I try to satisfy my own needs, I'll end up punished and embarrassed. I'm at the mercy of others, so I'll be good and conform.*

Another memory shows him trying to get his needs met.

"My dad and brother came home for lunch. I locked my-self in their car so they would have to take me with them. But I was scared, so I opened the door and ran away. They chased me and caught me. I felt afraid because I knew wouldn't get to go with them and I'd be punished."

Interpretation—*taking action to get my needs met will get me into trouble and won't work.*

There was also a memory that rewarded John's good behavior. "My aunt took me shopping with her. I sat still so long. I was very good while she tried on dresses. The store owner rewarded me by letting me choose a little gift to take home to my mother. I was surprised and thrilled!"

Interpretation—*if I sit still long enough, being good, people will approve of me, like me and reward me.*

John was religiously adhering to his early decision—sitting still, being good and waiting for people to like him and reward him. Only it wasn't working. He was in my office trying to discover what he was doing wrong. His memories were a gold mine of insight.

John experienced millions of incidents in the course of his life. There may very well have been some in which he asserted himself and something good happened. But he didn't remember those because they went against the belief system he'd begun to choose as a very young child. We often dismiss incidents that seem to deny our basic "truths" by labeling them as flukes or rare exceptions to the rule. Instead we keep the ones that prove the rule we've chosen.

I'm sure John had enjoyed a decent share of teachers' and parents' approval by sitting still, being good and not taking risks. So he got reinforcement for his beliefs. The more times your behavior "works" for you, the more sure you are you've got the right technique.

But what happens when tried-and-true methods no longer bring rewards? You crumble. You get discouraged and depressed. You continue using the methods you've clung to all these years, but you try *harder*. If you were John, you might sit more still and be better, but it would separate you even more from the real world. Finally you hurt so much you look around for some answers. Your life begins to change when you discover your mistaken beliefs and form new ones.

How to Change Beliefs

Early memories in this process provide direct insight into exactly how you can try to get your goals met. Once you interpret the memories, you can decide their appropriateness for yourself as an adult. You change them in fantasy so you can experience new feelings to accompany new behavior.

For example, as a child John probably acted wisely in complying with Aunt Molly's wishes to lie back down and go to sleep. But is it working for him now? No!

So John may give himself permission to decide for himself when he wants to lie down and sleep and when he feels like climbing out of his bed. John might picture himself in a crib now, at his present age. He can imagine someone who loves him coming in to suggest he lie down and go to sleep.

He can then imagine himself saying (or actually say aloud), "I know you have my best interests at heart, Aunt Molly, but I feel like getting up now. I have things I want to do." He'd further imagine himself letting down the crib side, hopping out, kissing Aunt Molly on the cheek and getting dressed for some fun.

"How would it feel to be able to do that?" I asked John.

His expression was one of delight. He replied, "It would feel great."

"Isn't it wonderful you have that power now?" I asked. "You have the right to make *all* those decisions. You can get up when you please, go to bed when you feel like it and respectfully ignore others' efforts to control your sleeping. *You* are the one in charge of your life!"

Obvious as that may be, it's amazing how frequently you don't realize you *are* in charge of your life. Many are still waiting for someone to let them out of the crib.

Let's look at another of John's memories. His parents drove up to the school, talked to the teacher and drove off leaving him upset and disappointed. He can also change that. First John might explore whether or not he did anything to attract his parents' attention. He probably didn't because he was so non-assertive. It's likely John stood quietly, waiting and being good.

That's an easy change to make. John could imagine himself waving his arms eagerly, jumping up and down, grinning and yelling, "Hi Mom and Dad!" He could make sure they noticed him.

"How would it feel, now, to deliberately invite attention?" I might ask. "Can you imagine the strength you'd feel getting your parents to respond to you? You no longer have to stand quietly and wait to be noticed.

"Taking it a step further, imagine yourself now seeing someone who's important to you or someone to whom you'd *like* to become important. Imagine that person driving slowly to a certain place. See yourself doing whatever it takes to attract that person's attention. How would it feel to watch that person's face light up when he recognized you?

"There *is* a risk. What if the person's face *didn't* light up? What if he looked angry at your behavior? Could you stand that? Absolutely. You wouldn't like it, but you could stand it just fine now that you're an adult. And you'd still enjoy the knowledge you had the courage to take a risk. That courage is what makes you strong and happy with yourself."

Courage is one of the most important concepts in everyone's life, yet people often reject it to avoid pain. Feeling hurt and/or rejected is so disconcerting some people do almost anything to avoid it. Inadvertently they cause themselves more pain than if they'd confronted the risk in the first place.

Like John did as a child, most of us find workable ways to avoid the discomfort of disapproval, even when those ways may be emotionally crippling to us. What does it take to reverse the process? It takes *courage* to do the things you fear.

John's memory of his fear on the playground is a good example of the same disabling fear he experiences now in social situations. He hoped he wouldn't be called to play a sport because he was so afraid of not knowing what to do. This shows his decision to avoid any possibility of embarrassment rather than risking, learning and growing.

Now he can go back to that playground in his mind and fantasize little John deciding to be courageous. He can allow himself to experience the fear of embarrassment. Instead of hoping he won't be chosen, he'd raise his hand and volunteer to play. Then he can imagine himself actually playing. He may fumble at first and feel uncomfortable with his ineptness, but he would gain confidence. It would be a huge step in experiencing courage in his present life.

From there it's only another step to imagining an office party John decides to attend. He can visualize himself walking over to a group of colleagues and becoming part of them, listening, lending a comment when it's appropriate.

There are unlimited ways to approach changing early memories. We've looked at some possible fantasy behavior changes John could make to help him feel strong. There are many additional avenues you can pursue that lead you in other directions and still get you in touch with the power of your untapped strengths.

One of those is changing an *attitude* in the early memory, rather than the *behavior*. Attitudes, beliefs and thoughts are the causes of all your feelings. Changing them automatically changes the feelings you experience.

Again using John's playground memory, he might explore his existing belief along with alternative beliefs he could adopt. "Being ignored or left out by people upsets me very much," was the belief I interpreted from the memory. How could he change his belief to one that would serve him more effectively both then and today as a grown man? Some possibilities include:

"Just because I go unnoticed sometimes doesn't mean I'm unloved or unimportant."

"If I don't receive the attention I want from one person, I can find positive ways to get it from someone else."

"I don't need *immediate* gratification. When I get home from school, I can find out what my parents were doing there."

"When I feel slighted or unfairly treated, I have the capacity to find something to do to change my direction from disappointment to happiness."

All these possibilities would help John begin to see himself as strong and capable, rather than weak and passive. His chief problem, non-assertiveness, made sense to him in light of his early memories and decisions. But now he's armed with new insights about his past and fortified with newly formed beliefs. He can begin the exciting climb to the freedom of choice he's never before experienced. He never knew he *had* so many choices in behavior or beliefs.

Creating New Beliefs

In the counseling process, we actually revise a person's beliefs on paper as part of the changing process. I elicit specific word changes from the person. John's first memory interpretation was "though I might want to climb out of my crib, I should lie down and go to sleep. I mustn't be assertive and adventurous. If I lie quietly and passively, people will love me."

John chose to change it to *I'm going to climb out of the crib and be assertive and adventurous. Then I can love and be loved even more.*

The second memory interpretation was "being ignored or left out by people upsets me very much. It's one thing I must try to avoid. I need their love."

John changed that to *being ignored or left out can upset me but only until I find something or someone else I can enjoy.*

His third decision was "I mustn't take risks. I'll avoid situations in which I might do badly because it's too horrible to feel embarrassed." It became *taking calculated risks will make me grow. Rather than avoid situations in which I might do badly, I'll confront them. Embarrassment is uncomfortable but not horrible; I know I can handle it.*

Another belief was "I hunger for companionship. I would be so happy if I could enjoy the company of a best friend, watching people, talking and laughing. I want that!" He amended it to *because I hunger for companionship, I will seek the company of friends. I want that, so I'll go after it!*

A fourth belief of John's was "I must always be obedient. If I try to satisfy my own needs, I'll end up punished and embarrassed. I'm at the mercy of others, so I'll be good and conform." It became *I needn't always be obedient. I must use my good judgment. Satisfying my own needs will make me happy. I'm in charge of my life and will consider my needs as well as others'.*

John also believed "taking action to get my needs met will get me into trouble and won't work." It became *taking action to get my needs met will usually help me achieve my goals and feel more fulfilled.*

The change John and I enjoyed the most was "if I sit still long enough, being good, people will approve of me, like me and reward me." He changed it to *sitting still and waiting will get me nowhere. I'll take social risks, enjoy the process and sometimes receive the reward of friendship.*

Chapter 7

Steps to Help You Interpret Your Lifestyle

I once had a client whose problem was *procrastination*. He couldn't get his life together, and he was angry at himself. In the course of our counseling, I found a wonderful tape designed primarily for people like Bob. I couldn't wait to lend it to him because I was sure he'd be as enthusiastic as I was and begin improving his life then and there.

"Call me when you've listened to it," I said as he left my office. He nodded agreeably. Five weeks later I finally called Bob.

"Well?" I asked. "What did you think of the tape?"

"I haven't listened to it yet," he admitted.

"What!!!" I exclaimed. "You haven't? Why not?"

"Because after the first 10 minutes, the speaker on the tape said to write down a list of our problems. I didn't have a pencil handy, so I shut the machine off and haven't gotten back to it."

I'm telling this story for a reason. Please don't hesitate

to finish reading this book, even if you don't feel like filling out the lifestyle questionnaire.

It's perfectly acceptable to enjoy reading it and never jot down one thing. You may not want to go to that much effort. Perfectionists often prefer not doing something at all to doing something imperfectly or incompletely. Perhaps you're like that. Or you may be reading this book the way I often read cookbooks—more for entertainment than for learning new skills.

Even if you don't fill out the questionnaire, you're bound to pick up some information that will give you insight into yourself and others. But for maximum self-understanding, you'll want to fill out and interpret the questionnaire.

Now for interpreting the questionnaire. First I have a counseling session with a client who has answered the questionnaire. Then I kick off my shoes and settle down on a comfortable couch with a cup of coffee and a colored pen. I write all my comments about his remarks in a bright color that stands out against the black print of his answers. The client can see clearly what he said, as well as my interpretation.

The interpretation is the most crucial part of the whole process, and it's *always* a matter of judgment. There is never a scientific, crystal-clear, absolute, correct answer, but the inherent meaning is usually fairly obvious.

The material you've read so far has given you information to help you interpret your own lifestyle questionnaire. Don't expect the expertise in yourself you might expect from an experienced counselor. But you've probably gained some new insights into your attitudes, expectations and beliefs just by reading the previous chapters. You'll be drawing on those insights as you look for meaning in your responses.

How to Interpret Your Questionnaire

Start with the adjectives describing each member of your family. In the previous section, we discussed how you generally appraise people for the values you prize or dislike. Begin by underlining any similar adjectives. (It's easier to see these if you use colored ink or a highlighting pen.)

Look for categories. Do you see words like "loving, caring, protective, kind" or "smart, responsible, achieving?" Underline "families" of similar words to help point up the importance of those values to you.

Write somewhere in the margin, "People should be" and list all the *positive* adjectives you've used to describe people. Follow that with a "People shouldn't be" column of the words that are *negative* in your estimation.

Next mark your name with an asterisk. Where you listed your own childhood adjectives, write "I am."

What you were as a child you probably still are. Occasionally people are very different now from whom they were as children. If you are, you'll know it. If you defined yourself as "sick, helpless, sad" as a child because of a physical disability that was corrected later on, you might have changed completely since then. In that case, you'll write some recognition of that reversal, such as "I was able to stop being" or "Traits I've rejected."

You know if you are a first, second, middle, youngest or only child. More than 4 years between siblings starts the birth-order characteristics all over again, beginning with another "first" child. Write down in the margin which child you are.

It's fun to attach a slogan to your birth position. Dr. Gary McKay, a Tucson counselor and author, taught me the slogans I used earlier to help define various personalities common to each category. (He credits some of them to Dr. Harold Mosak.) Some of the words may have gotten changed in the process, but here's a quick review.

First child's motto—*I was here first, and first I'll stay*.

Second child's motto—*I try harder!*

Middle child's motto—(anyone squeezed between others)—*Life is unfair*.

Youngest child's motto—*I'm entitled*.

Only child's motto—*I'm special*.

Write down the slogan for your birth position. If you fill two positions, like a second and a youngest, write down *both* slogans.

Go to the question about which family member was most like you and in what ways. Above your list of ways, write "I am." Circle the list. Above the list of ways in which someone was most different from you, write "I am not." Circle that list.

Next look at the question about how you got your way as a small child. Your childhood way is usually still your favorite way, so write before your answer "To get my way I . . ." Circle the entire statement.

Next to the list of compliments you received as a child, write "I am." Circle the list. Do the same thing with the list of negative criticisms unless you changed any trait. Then write "I'm no longer." Look at the phrase you'd like on your tombstone describing the way you'd like to be remembered. Beside it write "I try to be" (if you do) or "I'd like to be" if that's more accurate.

Circle the mottoes your mother and father would have hung over the kitchen sink.

Remember your favorite childhood story. Look for the essence of meaning in your favorite part of the story. Usually I write, "How life should be" next to that statement. Circle it.

Sometimes there is no real significance as far as story line. Occasionally someone likes a book because of the cute animal pictures or because someone special used to read it. In that case, don't do anything with it. One of the values of this questionnaire is there are many checks and double-checks. Every answer doesn't have to be meaningful. Leaving one or two responses blank won't matter because most of the others are meaningful.

Look at what animal you'd choose to be and why. The "why" answer is important. Write "How I'd like to be" in front of your answer. Circle the description.

The question about waving a magic wand to change anything about your childhood may or may not be relevant to your life today. If you answered something like, "I'd have had brothers and sisters so I'd have learned to get along with others better," circle that last phrase. Add "I wish I could."

If the wish seems to apply only to events of your childhood, like "Dad would have been less restrictive; more open and warm," ask yourself how that might affect your life now. Write that in. Perhaps you'd write "so I could have felt more comfortable with men" or whatever you think would have been the advantage of things being different then. Think about how early circumstances affected your life. Write your best interpretation. Circle your answer.

The question about what you'd change today is easy to interpret. Your answer is what you wish were different. It's a circumstance, situation or a person you'd like to change. It's a clearly stated problem you're currently trying to solve. Circle it.

Next look at the fantasy about hiding and overhearing two people talking about you. What thought did you think, overhearing their remarks? The *response* is what's important. Circle it, and circle the feeling you felt hearing that discussion. Write a sentence that summarizes the meaning behind your statement and your feeling.

Here's an example. Amy imagined hearing her mother say, "I'm concerned about Amy. She's awfully skinny."

Dad answered, "Hmph."

Amy's response was, "Mother cares about my well-being." Her feeling was *gladness*.

In interpreting this fantasy today, Amy might write down a statement like, "Being cared about makes me glad," or "I'm glad when people are concerned about me."

Here's another example. Cyndy imagined hearing her dad say, "Cyndy's going to be somebody when she grows up. I have a lot of faith in her."

Mom answered, "That's nice, dear."

Cyndy's response was, "Daddy's right. I am going to be somebody when I grow up." She felt *excited*. So she might write down, "Knowing I'm going to *be* somebody when I grow up is exciting."

The essence of your response is a very important life-style statement that you're probably still living today.

The last area to interpret is early memories. These are the most fun to look at, so take your time. Give each a lot of thought. Sometimes the main thrust of the incident jumps out at you, but other times you have to search for it. What you're looking for is the meaning behind the incident.

My friend and colleague, Dr. Maxine Ijams, suggests you imagine seeing the entire incident projected on a movie screen. Watch it happen. Which frame or scene of that "movie" is the most vivid in your mind right now? That's the part of the memory you'll want to underline.

Then identify the feeling you felt as that scene happened. The feeling must be one word, like "scared," "thrilled" or "angry." Phrases like "I felt like a star" or "I felt he shouldn't act that way" are not allowed. Those are judgments rather than feelings, so keep your feeling to just one word.

When you're interpreting the memory, consider the entire incident described. Zero in on the underlined sentence or phrase as the most important part. Sometimes it can give the whole incident an unexpected twist, like the client who remembered "getting hit by a car one day when I was out riding my new bike. I got knocked down, and the bike fell on top of me. I was lying there on the street in a puddle of blood. All the neighbors and my family came running out, looking scared for me. I felt thrilled with all the attention." What started out as a negative recollection was a positive one, thanks to the good feeling that highlighted the ending.

You're looking chiefly for three points:

1. The most vivid scene.
2. The feeling that occurred at that point.
3. The reason for that feeling.

For example, the client who got knocked off his bike might say, "The reason I felt thrilled was because of all the attention."

Good memories are "how life should be." Bad ones are "what I try to avoid in life."

Following are some examples of clients' early memories and my interpretations of them:

Carol's Early Memories	Lee's Interpretations
I was just a baby. <u>Mom was carrying me on her shoulders, singing a lullaby.</u> I felt (secure) because I knew I was loved.	Being carried on someone's shoulders shows love and caring. You can feel secure when you're being carried.

Grandpa had a wooden leg I loved. I begged him to let me polish it. He finally let me. I <u>polished it</u> all the time after that and felt so (happy) doing it for him.

"Polishing someone's wooden leg" makes me happy.

I beg people to let me do things for them.

My brother got spanked by Dad. I got angry at Dad because he hurt my brother. <u>I sat on the floor holding my brother, and we both cried.</u> He kept holding onto me. I felt (sad) but (glad) I could comfort him.

Seeing someone mistreated makes me angry.

When someone hurts, it makes me glad to comfort them, holding onto them and letting them keep holding onto me.

In fifth grade there was this real heavy boy named Tex. All the kids made fun of him. The man teacher was rough, and one day <u>he hit Tex across the hands with a paddle.</u> I felt so (sorry) for him I got up and kicked the teacher. Then I got paddled.

When I feel sorry for anyone in trouble or in need, I must intercede, even if I get hurt in the process.

My aunt and uncle were burned in a fire. She lived 6 days. All she did was cry for me. They finally let me into her room, but I couldn't touch her. <u>I just</u>

When I can't help someone who is hurting, I feel lost, awful and defeated.

stood there. She pointed to the wall, and her daughter got out a little lamb she'd bought for me. I felt awful, lost, defeated because I couldn't help her.

I was wrestling with my cousin on the living-room floor. When my aunt said stop, he said we'd go outside and play. He put me on his shoulders, and we went to the candy store. I came back with 75¢ worth of candy, still riding on his shoulders. I felt mischievous and happy because both my aunt and cousin were good to me.

Being carried off on someone's shoulders to buy candy makes me feel mischievous and happy.

I love it when people are good to me.

I had a big package under the Christmas tree from Jack and a small one from Jimmy. Jimmy always felt he couldn't compete with Jack. I opened the big one first—it was a big stuffed bear. Jimmy looked so hurt, but his present was a drum. I went marching around with it, wanting him to think I loved the drum.

My responsibility for other people's feelings prevents me from enjoying my own presents.

I felt ⟨sad⟩ and ⟨sorry⟩ for Jimmy because he felt so in-adequate.

I must do all kinds of things to try to make others happy.

Interpretation of Other Lifestyle Questionnaires

From these examples you may have guessed Carol is a champion "rescuer." She feels responsible for everyone's bad feelings. She feels lost, awful and defeated when she can't make them happy. She thrives on "polishing people's wooden legs." While it gives her great pleasure to "carry people on her shoulders," Carol longs to "be carried on theirs."

A part of Carol hungers to be the receiver of people's caring and love. But she's so good at being the benevolent giver/rescuer/nurturer, people tend to sit back and let her continue that role.

Realizing these feelings enabled Carol to make some decisions in her life. She began teaching her family and co-workers she'll always be nurturing, but she'd enjoy being nurtured as well.

Let's look at another example of how early memories point to your lifestyle decision. This time I'll tell you the client's "problem" ahead of time. According to his wife, "Mark runs away from his problems. He ignores them. He's a pleaser, but he's sneaky. I can't let my guard down. I'm forced to take all the responsibility, then he feels con-trolled."

According to Mark, "I love Hilda more than I've ever loved anyone. She says I hurt her by being selfish. She begged me not to go on a camping trip; I went anyway. I run away rather than confront her. I've given her all the responsibilities. I sit back and let her take over. I procrastinate."

At least they see eye to eye. Below are Mark's early memories and my interpretations.

Mark's early memories	Lee's interpretations
I was 3 or 4 years old. I went outside to <u>march with the high school band</u> as they practiced <u>in front of our house.</u> I (loved the freedom) of it. <u>Mom paddled me for it</u> though, and I was (sorry.)	I can't resist running out to march with the band! I love freedom but am sorry when I get punished for it.
A new girl came to our school. <u>We went to a movie.</u> I felt a (sense of accomplishment) because I'd made a new friend, and we enjoyed each other's company.	Making new friends gives me a sense of accomplishment. It's fun to enjoy people's company.
I don't have a specific memory about school. But I (liked) school because <u>I got to do a lot of playing and a lot of running around.</u>	I like situations where I get to do a lot of playing and a lot of running around.
Every day I got spanked by Mom for <u>running off.</u> I expected it after awhile. <u>I did it anyway</u> and felt (rebellious.) I was going to do what I wanted, no matter what.	I refuse to be controlled by anyone and will rebel if they try. I'm going to do what I want, no matter what.

You can see what Mark's early decisions were. "Life is a place where freedom is wonderful and worth the price of punishment. Making friends gives me a sense of accomplishment. It's fun to enjoy people's company. I like situations where I get to do a lot of playing and running around. I will defy anyone who tries to stop me."

However, if Mark truly loves Hilda as much as he says he does, he'll be willing to change some of those decisions to be more considerate of her. Changing a decision is the first step to changing behavior. Redeciding gives us a new chance at making relationships work.

But if Mark decides to keep his original decisions, *no one* will be able to make him change! Then Hilda must decide how she chooses to handle their relationship. Understanding early decisions helps each of them see clearly what obstacles they're trying to deal with.

Certainly this man is no wimp. Mark shows a great deal of strength as a consistent "doer." He is bound and determined to do his thing in spite of everyone else. His strength and determination will be his salvation in making whatever changes he wants to make in his life.

A doer is a person whose early memories are about doing something. (I threw the ball.) A receiver has something done to him. (She threw the ball at me.) An observer watches others do things. (I watched them play ball.) Examine your early memories again, and write by each one whether you were a doer, receiver or observer. Then write at the bottom of the page, "I tend to be" (whichever you were most).

The Next Step

Now that you've interpreted your lifestyle questionnaire, you're ready to list your beliefs. You've already done the hard part—thinking up answers to the questions and interpreting them in colored ink. Look for each comment you made in color; you use these important beliefs to define life.

You have millions of beliefs about all kinds of subjects. But you won't list all of them. Write down the ones that came from interpreting the lifestyle questionnaire. They are the key to the values you hold dearest.

It's significant that the most important values and beliefs are the ones that cause the most pain. Included in the 99,980 less-important beliefs are those like, "don't wear white shoes until Easter, eat an egg every morning, women should never go into bars alone, men should offer ladies their seats on crowded buses" and so on.

However, those beliefs don't usually upset you too much when you see them disregarded. The ones that cause stress when they're disregarded will probably be found in the list you write now. They're your Important Beliefs.

At the top of a sheet of paper write "My Beliefs." Follow that with, "Life is a place where . . ."

You probably have 15 to 30 sentences written in color from your interpretations of the lifestyle questionnaire. Write them on this page. Leave space between each one so you'll have room to make changes later.

To give you an example of a completed questionnaire, with interpretations and a list of beliefs, I'll use the one I did for my good friend Cyndy. She gave me permission to use it provided I spelled her name correctly and promised to include her phone number! (I think she was kidding about that.)

Cyndy is one of the cutest, brightest, most sparkly young women I've ever met. She is what we call "a princess." She feels very special and deserving of attention. She *is* special and *does* get a lot of attention. But she has trouble dealing with the dullness and "ordinariness" of her life. Below is her lifestyle questionnaire.

Cyndy's Lifestyle Questionnaire

1. List the names and present ages of your parents and siblings in the order of their birth. Include any who died and at what age. Write three words describing each one the way you saw him when you were a child.

Name	Age	Descriptive Adjectives		
Dad	__	big	strong	"The greatest"
Mom	__	nice	doesn't yell	my pal & confidante
Mickey	38	wonderful	funny	very smart
Shirley	33	pretty	indulged me	spoiled me
David	29	scared me	mean to me	strange
Tim	24	strange	loner	nonconformist
*Cyndy	22	I am (pretty	special	spoiled)
		(I manipulated people differently.)		

People should be: big, strong, great, nice, wonderful, funny, smart, my pal and confidante, spoil me and indulge me.

They shouldn't be: mean to me, strange, loners and scare me.

Youngest child's motto: I'm entitled.

2. **Of your parents and siblings, which one was (or is) most like you?** Mickey

In what ways?

I am a: *rebel without a cause; nonconformist; free bird.*

3. **Which one was most different from you?**
   David

In what ways?

I'm not a: *quiet, angry loner.*

4. **As a small child how did you go about getting your way?**

To get my way I'll: *throw temper tantrums.*

5. **What kinds of compliments did you receive as a child, from parents, teachers, family, friends?**

I am: *pretty, pretty, pretty.*

6. **What kinds of negative criticism did you receive?**

I am: *loud.*

7. **When you die (at age 100, at least!) what short, descriptive phrase would you like on your tombstone to describe you as you'd *like* to be remembered?**

"Uniqueness became her."

I try to be special and unique.

8. **If your mother had a sign over the kitchen sink to teach a strong value of hers, what would it have said?**

"You should never bother anyone."

9. **What would your father's sign have said?**

"Don't wear out your welcome."

10. **What was your favorite childhood story, book or fairy tale?**

A story Dad made up about a lady cop.

What was your favorite part of that story?

It *always had a happy ending.* (how life should be)

With whom did you identify?

Not her— I resented Dad's liking her better than me.

11. If you had to come back in another life as an animal, what would you choose to be? *A rabbit*. Why?

I am: *clever*.

12. If you could wave a magic wand and change anything or anyone about your childhood, what would you change?

People should be: *My father, to be more compassionate, less-restrictive, less-demanding*

13. With that same magic wand, what or whom would you change about your life right now?

I'd be more comfortable with myself, my faults and my high points.

14. What problems did you have in your childhood that you still have now?

Accepting compliments. I'm embarrassed being complimented, and yet I long for them.

15. Picture the house you lived in when you were a child. Imagine yourself playing in some secluded spot by yourself. Try to remember a specific place and actually "see" yourself there right now . . . perhaps in your bedroom, in a tree, behind a bush or out in the barn. Now picture two people who were important to you then—parents, friends, grandparents; any two you want to choose. What two people do you picture?

Mom and Dad.

Imagine you hear them talking about you, although they don't know you can hear them. One of them says:

Dad says, "Cyndy's going to be somebody when she grows up. I have a lot of faith in her."

The other responds:

Mom says, "That's nice, dear."

16. What thought do you think to yourself, overhearing their remarks?

Daddy's right. I am going to be somebody when I grow up.

17. And what feeling (one word) do you feel?
   Happy.

Cyndy's Early Memories	Lee's Interpretations
(Earliest) I was running down the hall on my birthday saying, "Mommy, Mommy, I'm 3 years old!" <u>My mother said only, "That's nice, dear."</u> I felt very ignored.	It's horrible being ignored when I feel so special!
	I don't get the recognition I deserve.
I was skipping along the sidewalk downtown, and <u>my father was skipping with me.</u> I felt very important.	I'm happiest when I feel very important.
	Men should skip down the sidewalk with me.
I fell out of a cherry tree. Dad came and picked me up. He was crying. I kept saying, "Don't worry about me, Daddy." He carried me into the hospital emergency room. I felt sorry for him.	I have compassion for people who hurt. I'm sorry for them.
	I'm very sensitive to others' feelings.

The next night Daddy woke me up and asked if I was hungry and wanted a peanut-butter-and-jelly sandwich. I said yes. He never got it for me. (Laughing) I've been waiting all these years. <u>He looked so worried.</u> I felt (very sorry) for him.

I'm still waiting for somebody to bring me my peanut-butter-and-jelly sandwich.

I was playing Monopoly with some relatives. Mickey made a deal with Ann that <u>I</u> wanted. I hit her. Everyone was shocked. I went off and brooded. <u>Ann came to talk to me, stroked my hair and said how nice I was and how good.</u> Then I felt (good,) and I felt (ashamed) I'd hit her.

I'll hit anyone who gets something I want, then I'll go off and brood. When I'm brooding, people should come talk to me, stroke my hair, tell me how nice I am and how good.

In third grade I glanced in as the boys' bathroom door opened. The boys told. I had to stand in the hall for three recesses. I was (devastated) <u>when the teacher confronted me</u> and felt (helpless) <u>I couldn't convince anyone it was an accident.</u>

Being punished or facing people's disapproval devastates me.

I feel helpless when I can't make people see things as *I* see them.

In second grade, I was talking during class. My teacher got <u>really</u> mad; hysterical! She made me stay in at recess. <u>She put my desk at a sunny window and said,</u> "<u>I hope you melt!</u>" I was (devastated.) I liked her. I <u>thought I must have been the most horrible thing ever born.</u> I felt (utter despair.)

Because I'm special, I should be allowed to talk when others can't.

People shouldn't get mad at me.

People's anger at me fills me with despair and devastation, especially when I like them.

The hard work is done. All we need to do at this point is write down comments and interpretations. I head the page:

Cyndy's Beliefs
(Life is a place where . . .)

- I'm entitled.
- People should be big, strong, great, nice, wonderful, funny, smart, pretty.
- People should never scare me, be mean to me, be strange or loners.
- Because I'm pretty, special and spoiled, I can manipulate people differently.
- I am a rebel without a cause, a nonconformist, free as a bird.
- I will never be a quiet, angry loner.
- To get my way, I'll throw temper tantrums.
- I'm pretty, pretty, pretty.

- Sometimes I'm loud.

- Uniqueness becomes me. I try always to be special, unique.

- You should never bother anyone.

- Everything should always have a happy ending.

- People shouldn't like anybody better than me.

- I'm clever.

- People should be compassionate with me, not restrictive or demanding.

- I'm embarrassed being complimented, yet I long for them.

- I am going to be somebody! I'm happy when people know that.

- It's horrible being ignored when I deserve recognition.

- I'm happiest when I feel very important.

- Men should skip down the sidewalk with me.

- I have compassion for people who hurt.

- I'm very sensitive to others' feelings.

- I'm still waiting for someone to bring me my peanut-butter-and-jelly sandwich.

- I feel sorry for someone who worries about me.

- I'll hit anyone who gets something I want, then I'll go off and brood.

- People should come talk to me, stroke my hair and tell me how nice and how good I am.

- Being punished or facing people's disapproval devastates me.

- I feel helpless when I can't make people see things as *I* see them.

- Because I'm special, I should be allowed to talk when others can't.

- People shouldn't get mad at me.

- People's anger at me fills me with despair and devastation, especially when I like them.

There you have Cyndy's complete lifestyle. The next step, which I'll illustrate by continuing the story of Cyndy, is to look over the person's beliefs and get his or her comments about the whole thing. When I go over the interpretations with a client, I always stress these are only *my* interpretations and not official proclamations carved in stone. "If you disagree with any of these, we'll take your word over mine," I tell the client. "You know yourself better than I do."

Some people take exception to a few beliefs on their list. But most nod agreeably and concur those beliefs seem pretty much true for them.

Cyndy did. So when I explained the next step, changing any of the beliefs she sees a need to change, she responded with surprise. "Do I *have* to change any?" she asked plaintively.

"Well, no, you don't have to," I assured her, "if you're happy with them as they are. But aren't there some that complicate your life? Let's read them again one by one and discuss each one."

So we read them again. After each sentence, I looked at her questioningly. She'd say, "I like that belief the way it is." Finally she did agree to change one. "*To get my way I'll throw temper tantrums*" became "*To get my way I'll bring myself to calmly and rationally communicate my feelings and listen and try to understand the other person's feelings."*

The next one she changed was *"It's horrible being ignored when I deserve recognition."* Because I strongly believe the language we use has a lot to do with our state of mind, I suggest people consider using less-dramatic language. "It's horrible" sounds pretty awful. Would she consider, "It's uncomfortable?" Yes, she would. So we scratched out "horrible" and wrote "uncomfortable" instead.

We continued looking at beliefs. Cyndy wanted to keep most of them. Even when I made what I thought were wonderful suggestions, she'd laugh and say, "No, I *want* to believe that."

"Men should skip down the sidewalk with me?" I read aloud. "You really believe that?"

"Well, maybe not literally, but in spirit, yes. Fun, lighthearted togetherness. I want that."

Now this is very unusual! People generally want to change many of their beliefs. Cyndy is one of the few clients I've ever had who genuinely liked most of hers and chose to keep them even though she knew they brought her some disappointment.

I was delighted when we came to another belief she agreed to change. *"I'll hit anyone who gets something I want, then I'll go off and brood."* She changed it to *"When anyone gets something I want, I may be uncomfortable, but I can handle it."*

In *"Being punished or facing people's disapproval devastates me"* she changed the word *"devastates"* to *"makes me uncomfortable."* To be devastated means one is almost unable to cope. To be uncomfortable may be unpleasant, but it certainly is tolerable. Anyone can stand discomfort.

The only remaining belief Cyndy chose to change was *"I feel helpless when I can't make people see things as I see them."* She replaced *"I feel helpless"* with *"It's OK."*

Much value in counseling comes from simple conversation about specific beliefs that are helpful or harmful. Every belief you have applies to some facet of your life. Most of them are directly responsible for any problems you face.

But often we cling to them for dear life. Perhaps it's because change is scary. The old maxim, "Better the devil you know than the devil you don't," applies here.

Some people say they want to change practically every belief. They go through their list quickly, eagerly crossing out words and phrases. They determine they're going to be new people before the day is through. Then they go home and remain exactly the same.

At least Cyndy is honest. She knows how difficult it is to change her lifelong wishes. She chooses to hold onto them even though she laughs at her perverse tenacity.

I reread *"People should come talk to me, stroke my hair and say how nice and good I am."* I said with mock sternness, "Now come on, Cyndy. Isn't that fighting a losing battle? People are not going to do that very often, are they?"

She twinkled and answered, "Maybe not, but I still think they should." After all, a princess *is* a princess.

Cyndy and I did her lifestyle questionnaire and interpretation 4 years ago. She's moved across the country since then. When I called her to ask her permission to use her lifestyle, the phone rang a few times before it was answered. A petulant, childlike voice said a thick, "Hullo?" I thought it might be a teenaged babysitter with a cold.

"This is Lee Schnebly. Is Cyndy there?"

"Leeeeee! Hiiii!" Immediately Cyndy's voice was happy,

clear and excited.

"Are you all right? You sound like something's wrong," I said.

"Oh, you know me," she said. "I'm just being a princess." She explained her husband had to work, and it was Sunday. She wanted him to spend the day with her. Apparently she'd been enjoying a bit of self-pity because clearly his working went against almost every belief on her list. He should have been there stroking her hair and telling her how nice and good she was. He should have been skipping down the sidewalk with her.

But she was laughing at herself as we talked. She sees her beliefs as unrealistic. But it's difficult for her not to give into them. She continues to try; that's all anyone can do. Cyndy's young, and I have no doubt every year will find her a little less unrealistic. In the process, she'll continue to be effervescent and delightful most of the time, with setbacks only when she feels ignored, overlooked or not properly appreciated.

Katie's Lifestyle Questionnaire

Following is an example of how Katie changed some of her beliefs. First, let's look at Katie's early memories and my interpretation of them. This exercise is followed by Katie's new beliefs.

Katie's Early Memories
Dad put me in first grade. I was <u>confused, bewildered and scared</u> because only my dad was there, but he did the best he could. <u>I walked in with my pigtails, very quiet,</u> (helpless and

Katie's Early Memories
I'm the receiver of action I don't like.

scared) because I didn't know what to expect.

I must passively accept whatever happens, feeling helpless and scared.

Playing in a garden, I'd wander around and pretend things. Alone, sometimes lonely. Sometimes I'd get lost in pretending. I felt good) when I pretended I was someone else.

It feels good to get lost in pretending, wishing I were someone else.

Life is more pleasant if I escape or withdraw.

When my stepfather drank, he did crazy things. One day he got a rifle and loaded it. I hung onto it. He couldn't get it away from me. I felt fear because he was threatening to shoot us all.

When I'm faced with a really serious situation, I'll act wisely and with great strength, even though I'm afraid.

My stepfather was drunk, driving in traffic as fast as he could go. I put my arms around his neck and said, "I love you. Please don't go so fast." He wouldn't slow down. I felt fear.

I'm a helpless victim of other people's bad behavior. I try to get them to cooperate with me by being sweet and loving, but it doesn't do any good. I'm afraid, and I can't control them.

I'm ineffectual at solving problems.

My grandmother loved me. When she cooked, I'd hold her around her waist real tight. It felt so good; I felt warm, safe and loved.

I'm happiest being loved, holding someone around the waist real tight.

It feels good to be warm, safe and loved.

One day she let me make bread. I felt good accomplishing something with her. I felt good because Grandpa told me how good the bread was.

It's good to accomplish something.

I like having skills other people appreciate.

I had to go from Mom's to Dad's. I didn't understand at all. Driving to Dad's in Mom's car, I felt hurt and sad, not wanting to go.

Even when I don't understand, and I'm hurt and sad, I have to do what I don't want to do.

I'm a helpless victim.

The problem Katie must lick is dependency. She sees herself as a helpless victim right from her earliest memory: "Dad *put me* into first grade." Her childhood decision to simply accept whatever happens, unable to change it for the better, has followed her into adulthood. Feeling ineffectual at solving problems, she chose to escape or withdraw when too uncomfortable. Longing for the love and security of Grandmother, she tried finding someone to "hold around the waist real tight," and would try to be sweet and loving to earn their cooperation. But dependency pushes people away rather than bringing them closer. Katie continued to feel hurt, sad and helpless.

Out of six memories, however, one was beautifully

strong—the one in which she prevented her stepfather from shooting the family. Even in the face of grave danger, she was able to use her wits and be heroic in spite of the nearly crippling fear she must have felt.

One memory like that is what I call "money in the bank." To know you've had strength and courage that overpowered justifiable fear can be reassuring in dealing with current fears and anxieties. If that strength was there once, it's available still.

Katie will always have the choice to escape from pain (she used alcohol to accomplish this) or to meet it courageously and confront the problem. Last time I talked to her, Katie was attending AA meetings and working on developing independence and pride in herself.

Katie's New Beliefs
(Life is a place where . . .)

- People don't know what I need, *unless I tell them*.

- They don't pick me up, talk to me, have time for me, want me around, *and I don't need them to*.

- I've very quiet, shy and confused, non-assertive. *but I'm becoming more assertive*.

- ~~I don't know~~ *I'm learning* to assert myself.

- Some people are self-sufficient, strong, capable, kind and loving, *and I can be, too*.

- Life ~~should~~ *can* be happy—~~a~~ *no* prince ~~should~~ *can* take me to his castle and make me happy ever after! *I'm responsible for my own happiness*.

- People love me, *if they want to*.

- I can't stand anyone's disapproval or rejection.

🔹 I ~~must~~ *can't* please everyone. *so I won't try.*

🔹 ~~Don't~~ *It's OK to* make waves. *I don't have to* Be passive, non-assertive.

🔹 ~~I have~~ *Everyone has* expectations that don't get met. *and I must be prepared for that.*

🔹 I'm ~~a~~ *sometimes a* helpless victim of others' behavior. *but I can cope with it in many ways.*

🔹 ~~I try~~ *Trying* to earn people's cooperation by being sweet and loving. *often doesn't work.*

🔹 I'm ~~ineffectual at~~ *capable of* solving problems.

🔹 I'm happiest being loved, holding someone around the waist real tight. *and I can be happy without that, too.*

🔹 It feels good to be warm and safe and loved.

🔹 I'm happiest accomplishing something.

🔹 ~~I'm~~ *I don't have to be* helpless, sad, have to do what I don't want to.

🔹 I'm *sometimes* the receiver of action I don't like, a victim. *but I can handle it.*

🔹 ~~I'll~~ *I won't* accept treatment I don't like and feel helpless and scared.

🔹 Life is more pleasant if I ~~"escape" or withdraw.~~ *confront and solve my problems.*

🔹 It feels good to get lost in pretending, wishing I were someone else. *but it's a waste of time.*

🍃 When I'm faced with a really serious situation, I'll act wisely and with great strength even if I <u>am</u> afraid.

Your Beliefs

What you do with your list of beliefs is exactly what Cyndy and Katie did with theirs. Read each one. Give some thought to how that belief is affecting your life.

🍃 Is it good for you?

🍃 Is it realistic?

🍃 Does holding onto that belief condemn you to further disappointments?

🍃 Does it keep you dependent on others?

🍃 Do you have freedom to make your own decisions?

🍃 How might the belief hold you back from risking and truly living life?

🍃 Does it give you something to hide behind while you continue to misbehave or be irresponsible?

🍃 How does it help you?

🍃 How does it hurt you?

It might be helpful to talk your beliefs over with someone else. Often it's difficult to see your choices and decisions clearly. If you have a close friend or significant other who's interested in doing a lifestyle, you could be very helpful to each other as sounding boards.

While some experts believe it's very difficult to interpret your own lifestyle, I believe you can do a pretty good job of it. At least it gets you thinking along certain lines. It makes you question your behavior and the beliefs behind it.

Chapter 8

There
Are Ways to
Change Your Beliefs

You've finished the lifestyle questionnaire. You've remembered and you've projected. You've clarified, interpreted, discussed, pondered, searched your soul and finally decided on changes you'd like to make. *Now* what do you do?

This stage is the starting point of a long-term plan. Don't expect to be a new person by next Tuesday or even in 6 weeks. But do expect to feel a sense of excitement at discovering new behaviors trickling into your life. Nothing succeeds like success. Each little victory will make the next one come more easily.

The idea is gradually to become a "new, improved" person. You've spent a lot of years making yourself into the person you are now. You did it by basing your thoughts, feelings and behaviors on the various beliefs you created over the years.

What you taught yourself you can reteach. You can replace old, tired, no-good thinking with fresh, new think-

117

ing. Unlike a table you've built, a dress you've stitched or a poem you've written, you're never "finished." Actually, you're probably somewhat different now from the way you were when you began reading this book. Change has already begun, unless you've disagreed with and rejected every thought you've read. If that were the case, you probably would have stopped reading a long time ago.

Much of your future change will take place almost by itself, as your early decisions took place. As a small child, you rarely identified your lessons in life as newly acquired beliefs. You simply picked them up and continued using them. That's what you'll do with these abridged beliefs. You'll gradually increase your awareness of them as you make small changes in behavior.

One of my early decisions was, "I must avoid anything scary." When I deliberately changed it to, "I will do the things I fear to do," I didn't go about looking for scary things to try. But life being what it is, scary things find me with some regularity.

I've never been comfortable with heights. I've told you about my San Francisco friend who "had to" go over the bridge. The fact she saw it as a "get to" was unthinkable to me.

A few years ago I heard about a brick factory in Tucson with great prices if you bought direct from their plant. I wanted to build a brick planter in our patio. I also love a bargain. So early one Saturday morning I set out to buy my bricks. I drove for miles before I came to Houghton Road. I drove for many more miles before I came to the general area that had to include the brick place.

Suddenly I rounded a curve. There, just ahead of me, was a bridge. Not just a bridge, but a *bridge!* It seemed to go way, way up in the sky. I was horrified to realize I had to drive across it if I wanted the bricks. Immediately I felt an anxiety attack starting—racing heart, sweaty palms, flushed face. I pulled off the deserted road and turned off the ignition so I could appraise the situation.

First of all, I was alone. I hadn't told anyone where I was going. I was afraid if I drove onto the bridge and got panicky, I might crash through the guard rail and plunge to an untimely death. No one would ever know! I felt I couldn't risk it.

But I'm a certified mental health-counselor who tells people to "do the thing you fear to do." I had to ask myself if I was actually going to turn around and go home without practicing what I preached. My shameful answer was, "Yes."

"You mean to say," I confronted myself, "you're a stone's throw from the brick factory, you've driven for 45 minutes and you're going to go home brickless?"

"You got it," I replied.

"You call yourself a counselor, yet you don't have what it takes to drive over a measly bridge?"

Before I was forced to answer me, a car came from the other direction. It sailed over the bridge as easy as pie.

"Hmm," I thought. "He made it."

"So *you* do it."

"Nope. It's too dangerous."

Just then another car came sailing across. "She did it," I acknowledged.

"But I can't."

I started the engine and made a quick U-turn toward home. But something made me stop. I sat there for a few minutes, looking at the evil structure in my rear-view mirror.

Suddenly I thought, *"Do it!"* Before I could change my mind, I turned around and sailed over the bridge!

You can't believe how thrilled I was, unless perhaps you've done the thing you feared to do sometime in your life. I drove over in a state of complete, ecstatic pride. I bought the bricks and coming back I approached the bridge as if it were nothing.

"*I* go over bridges," I thought to myself smugly. "Nothing scares *me*, by golly."

Now if you happen to be a Tucsonan who has driven down Houghton Road you might be thinking, "*That* little bridge? She was scared of *that?*"

Fears are like that. To the unafraid they seem incomprehensible. But to the fearer, they are no small matter.

I take comfort in the fact everyone has some kind of fear. If you have no fears at all, you're extremely unusual. If you have some, you get to have the fun of attacking them by "doing the thing you fear to do."

I learned that thought from a wonderful self-help group called *Recovery, Inc.* It was started in the 1930s by a psychiatrist who saw the need for people to help people. Dr. Abraham Low began with a handful of his patients and saw the group become so successful it branched out to cities all over the world.

I thoroughly recommend finding a Recovery group in your community if you want to learn more about their methods. I suggest you go more than just once. Any new technique seems strange at first. Joining a group where everyone already seems to know each other might make you feel like an outsider. But so what? It's only temporary. In the half hour of social time that follows the meeting, you can meet everyone and chat about anything you feel like exploring.

I attended weekly Recovery meetings for 2 years. I learned so many helpful phrases I don't remember them all. But I still think of many of them frequently, usually when I'm stressed about something. My favorites are "do the thing you fear to do" and "it's distressing but not dangerous."

It's Distressing But Not Dangerous

Most of the things that upset us, when you stop and think about them, are *not* dangerous. They are simply distressing. Often we attach danger to situations or circumstances that, in reality, are just distressing and quite tolerable. Recognizing that trait in ourselves can help us become aware of the times we do it, which is the first step in changing our behavior.

Applying the idea of "distressing but not dangerous" to our lifestyle beliefs makes it easier to come up with appropriate changes, such as:

Old Belief: Speaking in public terrifies me.

New Belief: It's distressing but not dangerous. Public speaking is uncomfortable, but I can do it.

Old Belief: I can't stand disapproval.

New Belief: It's distressing but not dangerous. I don't like disapproval, but I can stand it.

Old Belief: I'm afraid of my husband's anger.

New Belief: It's distressing but not dangerous. My husband's anger won't hurt me. It's just unsettling.

Old Belief: I don't dare disagree with my mother-in-law.

New Belief: It's distressing but not dangerous. It's OK to disagree with my mother-in-law.

Old Belief: I'm scared to ask the boss for a raise.

New Belief: It's distressing but not dangerous. I have the courage to ask my boss for a raise.

These situations might be disconcerting, anxiety provoking or uncomfortable, but they're *not* dangerous. Yet we often treat them as if they were. An exception would be if your husband, mother-in-law or boss were into physical violence and might beat you up during a confrontation. But the chances of that happening are very slim.

We usually fear the uncomfortable feelings we would experience during a confrontation. Because the situations that shake us up emotionally are usually the causes of most of our stress, it's very freeing to incorporate the line, "distressing but not dangerous" into our lives.

Have the Will to Bear Discomfort

Another one of Recovery's good lines is, "have the will to bear discomfort." This doesn't mean you're supposed to go around seeking out uncomfortable situations. But you should know you can tolerate them when they arise. We seem to think we shouldn't be expected to bear discomfort. Discomfort is so uncomfortable we don't want to have to endure it. But we do, and so does everyone else.

I remember wailing to a psychiatrist one time, "But I have so many problems!" I was surprised when he looked at me a bit incredulously and said with some annoyance, *Everybody* has problems."

"They do?" I thought. That was the first I knew of it. I'd always thought it was just me.

Now I know problems are par for the course. When one arises, I have to be willing to bear some discomfort to solve it. No pain, no gain.

But what many of us do is run from discomfort so fast we create all kinds of other problems in addition to the one we're running from. It would be so much simpler and more effective to stay and confront the original problem head-on.

That's when it's helpful to remind ourselves, "I have the will to bear discomfort." It's another way of saying, "I can stand it. So what if it hurts? I'm no baby."

I wish I had thought of that phrase the morning I was trembling by the side of the bridge. It might have helped me make the decision to "do it" a little sooner.

I believe every time you run from something threatening or discomforting, you grow more timid and less confident in every way. Conversely, you can meet a challenge, face a fear, have the courage to do the thing you fear to do. You know it's distressing but not dangerous, and you grow stronger.

Change May Mean Courage

What "change" seems to amount to is simply old-fashioned *courage*. Having courage to face things you fear is the key that unlocks the door to freedom. You can cower in the corners of the prisons you've built in your mind. Or you can conjure up your courage and do what you fear to do. It all boils down to your own choice.

I used to have a rubber tree in a giant pot in our living room. It dropped leaves and looked sickly. No amount of plant food could make it stand up and look happy. One day I took a sample leaf to the man at the nursery. I asked if he could diagnose its illness.

"Sure," he said. "It doesn't have good drainage. I'll bet you water it and let the water sit in the bottom."

"I have to," I said. "It's a great big pot. There's no way I could lift it to drain the water."

"Well, lady," he said brusquely, "either you drain the pot when you water the plant, or you watch the plant die. It's your choice." And he walked away.

I judged him insensitive, unsympathetic and unhelpful.

Didn't he understand I couldn't possibly lift the pot, and I didn't want to move it outside? I went home and stewed about it for a while, studied it often and watched the plant wither and die over the next few months. It was my choice, and I chose badly.

I think of that rubber tree occasionally when I'm faced with a choice of doing what I should do to grow or cowering in my safe corner. Choosing *not* to do the thing I fear makes my roots get sodden, soggy and moldy, like the rubber tree's. My emotional leaves wither and fall.

Choosing to *do* the thing I fear keeps me growing new shoots and nice, glossy leaves. Unquestionably, the key is courage.

Acting "As If"

While you're being courageous and beginning new behavior, you can add another attitude to help you attain changes you're working toward. You can act "as if."

Acting "as if" is helpful in the process of change. New behavior is usually slightly artificial and may feel unnatural at first. But pretending you're already "there" helps you get there. Acting "as if" is a useful tool in changing any habit or behavior you want to change.

When I was a little girl, my mother frequently admonished me to "stand up straight." Sometimes she straightened out my slumping shoulders and even demonstrated how to stand—tummy in, shoulders back, head up. I dutifully imitated her but not for long. Good posture was not one of *my* values, though obviously it was one of hers. The fact she mentioned it relatively often seemed to prove I did have bad posture. That became one of the facts about myself I stored away as my unconscious self-definition.

Not long ago I was looking at some recent snapshots of my family. I became uncomfortably aware my shoulders looked droopy and tired in every picture. I hated the idea I was beginning to look "bent" and aging. Suddenly, at 54, posture became a value.

I remembered all the times I'd told clients to act "as if." Could I act "as if," even with a physical characteristic that had been with me for over 50 years? I decided I had nothing to lose. Then and there I straightened my shoulders and said for the first time, "I'll act as if I have good posture."

After that, I must have said it to myself two dozen times a day. I wish I could say my shoulders stayed up like magic once I'd made that decision. But more often than not, I found myself slumped comfortably in my chair as I listened to clients. But now there was a new awareness. Everyone, including me, knew I didn't stand up straight. I slumped—always had, always would. Except now I knew a secret. I didn't have good posture, but I could act as if I did.

I can't tell you what the difference was, but gradually I began to feel different. Because it was a secret with myself, I wasn't risking failure in the eyes of the people around me. I'm really not sure of all the dynamics involved, but the set of my shoulders has definitely changed a little.

My newfound skill was rather heady and exciting. I began looking for ways to share it with clients.

"I wish I got along better with my dad," a client told me not long ago. He was a 25-year-old man caught up in a lifetime quarrel with his dad. Though he was married, capable, a father of two children and a very pleasant person to be around, he seemed to change in his father's company. At family gatherings, the two of them ended up trading insults or at least dirty looks. Clearly they both knew their roles in life, which was not to get along.

I suspect both of them felt bad about it. I know the son did. I suggested my act-as-if method. We talked about how his life would be different if he were more comfortable with his father.

He really wanted to be. He was tired of seeing the disappointment on his mother's face when the family get-together turned sour because of the father-son upset. He was angry with himself for his inability to control his behavior. He dreaded the guilt he knew he'd feel someday when his father died. He *wanted* to change.

That's the first step. If he hadn't wanted to change, no amount of useful skills would have been effective. But because he wanted to get along with his father, he took my suggestion and began acting as if they were friends. His father responded eagerly. Today they get along quite well, with only an occasional argument. This all came about because my client acted as if the relationship were already as friendly as he wanted it to be.

We are very strong when it comes to behaving exactly the way we want to behave. If we truly desire a change in behavior or personality, the act-as-if method is a wonderful step in the right direction.

My daughter Lisa and I have always considered ourselves "compulsive eaters." We struggle valiantly to avoid fattening foods only to run impulsively to the kitchen and consume an entire bag of cookies. We lose 3 pounds and gain them back. We starve, then feel sorry for ourselves and eat chocolate. We are absolute experts on calories and food values. It is not a lack of knowledge that makes us gain weight. Rather, it is some complex process of emotionalism that makes food a "reward" when we "deserve" something. Often we "deserve" it simply because we've deprived ourselves of it.

Many times I've been at meetings where refreshments are served. Most of the time I take a cup of coffee or tea and pass up the cookies or breads. I feel noble, strong and disciplined watching the others enjoy their food. But sometimes I also feel deprived and self-pitying.

When I'm trying to watch my calories, I might eat a salad for lunch and just a touch of carbohydrate to round it off nutritionally. But by 4:00, I'll be thinking, "At least I deserve *this,*" as I spread peanut butter thickly on toast.

In light of the extreme amount of thought and effort Lisa and I expend to fight the battle of weight, we've managed to stay relatively slender. But it's been a constant battle for many years.

Recently Lisa and I were having dinner together at a salad bar, discussing our mutual problem. We commiserated for probably the millionth time how tough it is to be so aware of food. We agreed we have a preoccupation with it that non-foodaholics couldn't possibly understand.

Suddenly Lisa said, "I wonder what would happen if we switched our thinking. What if we began saying, I'm the kind of person who can eat what I want and not gain weight?"

As she pursued that idea, I began to get excited. I realized it's exactly what I always recommend to clients. But I'd never thought of it with eating habits.

My entire life has revolved around food. The family recounts the fact my coloring books from childhood had all pictures of food colored in and not much else. Larry observed years ago with some amusement that I read cookbooks the way some men read porno magazines.

My first question to the children when they'd come home from a party was always, "What did they have to eat?" When they began to kid me about it, I asked it less, but I still wondered.

I always felt deprived in situations that included food. I almost never felt, "There now, that's enough. I feel full and content." Rather it was, "Now you have to stop. You can't eat anymore," like a stern parent giving unwelcome orders to an enthusiastic child. I'd stop, but the rebellious child in me mumbled, "I've got a reward coming to me for this."

Since our discussion that evening, Lisa and I are brainwashing ourselves. We agreed to tell ourselves as often as we can remember that food is not an issue with us. Saying things like, "I could eat that if I wanted to, but I don't want it right now," is beginning to make me think like a "normal" person who is not obsessed with food.

"There is an abundance of food. I can have some of that any time I want."

"I'm not hungry right now."

"There are so many things I'd rather do than eat."

What we're doing is acting "as if." I'm positive it will re-structure our self-images if we continue it long enough. Everything we know about ourselves we learned some-where along the way. So all we're doing is learning new facts about ourselves by conscious programming.

I imagine how it must feel to be a thin person who doesn't use food as recreation. A thin person uses food as a pleasant refueling of the body. What phrases would that person say and think? And I say and think them to myself.

How does this concept of acting "as if" fit in with my belief in the need for honesty? I'm doing it as an honest approach to facilitate changes I desire in myself. I'm try-ing something new in attacking an old problem. Pretend-ing is fun and harmless, as long as I'm honest about doing it. The only time pretending can be dangerous is when I use it to deceive myself, acting one way and feeling another, without admitting the feelings.

I see this method as similar to the game I used to play with the kids when they were small. If we were eating fish sticks at our breakfast bar, I might say, "Let's play like we're eating at Anthony's in San Diego! Can you imagine the sun sparkling on the water and a harbor cruise boat sailing by?" We pretend. Before long, we are!

The process of acting "as if " is an ongoing one, rather than one that creates an immediate personality change. Think of it as an intriguing game to play lightheartedly, with interest. If you constantly measure progress, it becomes just another kind of tyranny you impose on yourself, probably doomed to failure.

When you notice progress in some of your thoughts or behaviors, enjoy it. But be prepared for old habits to stick with you for some time. Gradually they will move out of the way for the new ones you're superimposing.

Change is good for everyone. It forces us to grow. Maybe that's why we fight it so hard. Few people actually welcome change, unless it's something they've carefully planned and worked toward or hoped for. Most people change reluctantly. I once read, "Life is what happens to us while we're busy making other plans."

Encouraging Yourself and Others

It's difficult to change beliefs, behavior or thoughts. You need to be extra kind to yourself to help the process along. You need to encourage yourself.

There is a chapter on encouragement in my first book, *Out Of Apples?*, which, needless to say, is excellent. See how good I am at encouraging myself? There are several excellent books on encouragement that give specific suggestions for "turning people on." My friend, Lew Losoncy, has spent a lifetime teaching people about encouragement. He maintains that every time two people get together, they each walk away feeling turned off or turned on. You can turn people on by believing in them and their abilities. Or you can turn them off by discouraging them and pointing out their mistakes and flaws.

Encouraging yourself is as important as encouraging others. You need it! It's easy to get discouraged by many factors in your life. Everyone needs an almost-constant source of encouragement to cope. Who is better qualified to see all the good qualities you have than yourself?

It makes sense, yet it feels strange. You may be lavish and sincere in pointing out friends' and family's strengths. But often you take your own for granted, if you're even aware of them at all.

The insights in this book are good starters in your quest for greater happiness. But the most important part of all may be the idea of encouraging yourself as you progress.

A surgeon was impressing on me the need for self-examination for breast lumps. He said, "No one is as capable as you in noticing even the slightest change in yourself. You have a great advantage over any doctor because you can feel yourself from the inside as well as the outside."

That also applies to encouraging yourself in your emotional health. Others see you only from the outside. They can't appreciate all the efforts you may be making inside your head. It's up to you to recognize those efforts and applaud yourself for them.

Dealing with Mrs. Mean

The kinder you are to yourself, the faster you'll progress. I've conjured up an exercise that helps me bring out the best in me. It might be helpful to you.

Everyone has two influential people inside their heads—one nice and one not so nice. The not-so-nice one always criticizes you. You can never measure up to his or her standards no matter how hard you try. Picture a composite of people in your life, present or past, who were bossy, non-approving, disagreeable and controlling. Use that image to help imagine the not-so-nice person. In my head, I picture a woman I refer to as "Mrs. Mean."

Mrs. Mean has become the conglomerate of all the people in my life who disapproved of my behavior. It was usually for my "own good." These disapproving people may have gone to their reward years ago, but they live on in my head, continuing to put me down. Mrs. Mean "catches" me overeating or doing a half-baked job at something. She tears me to ribbons for my behavior. Even if I could be a paragon of virtue every minute of the day but one, she'd descend on me with fury for that small lapse.

The Mrs. Mean in my head begins scolding me the minute I wake up in the morning. She uses critical, negative statements.

"OK, get on the scale. You'll see why you shouldn't have eaten that cinnamon roll yesterday. See? See that extra pound? (triumphantly) I told you when you were looking at it in the refrigerator you shouldn't eat it. Did you listen? No. You're too dumb and too stubborn to listen to good advice. That's just one of your problems. I try to whip you into shape, but you ignore me. So here you are, a pound heavier. You're going to end up fat, fat, fat! You'll deserve every miserable minute of it. Sure, head right for the kitchen and more food. Is that all you think about? You should be in there working on your book. How many more excuses are you going to find to put it off? You're lazy. You can find time to watch TV, but what about time to call your neighbor in the hospital? Not you. Selfish, self-ish woman. Look at that dust on the table. When are you going to give this house the cleaning it needs? It's only needed it for a year. You run here and there, giving it a lick and a promise now and then. What kind of wife are you? A lazy one, that's what. . ." And so on, ad nauseum.

She's relentless. She's so aggressive she makes herself present in any situation, invited or not. You know the worst thing? I listen to her as if she were important and I needed the information she's giving me. In truth, that's not the case.

No one likes to be bossed around. We're all good at defeating the controller. We become rebellious when we're pushed, nagged and criticized. The more Mrs. Mean tries to whip me into shape, the more determined I be-come to do exactly what she tells me I can't. Like a little kid refusing to do something I'd really enjoy, I stoutly re-sist simply to defy Mrs. Mean.

If Mrs. Mean had any sense at all, she'd shut up and let me pursue my goals and values on my own. I'd certainly do a better job alone than I do with her watching me for mistakes.

Send your Mrs. Mean away on a long vacation. She's earned one. She's been working like a dog all her life to make you perfect, and she's been a failure. No one is per-fect. Buy her a one-way ticket to Australia. Once you're rid of her, get to know another person who lives inside your head.

Meet Mrs. Mellow

Now picture someone who's the opposite of Mrs. Mean. This person is a composite of all the kind, loving, gentle people who believed in you. Just the tone of this person's voice gives you a lift. You're drawn to her because she always makes you feel good about yourself. She sees your mistakes or faults, but she has a way of looking at them that's different from Mrs. Mean.

The lady I call "Mrs. Mellow" is a conglomerate of nurturing parent, encouraging teacher, lighthearted friend and anyone else extremely positive in my life. You've known people like that; you'd probably do anything to help them out. Encouraging people brings out the best in you. You have nothing to rebel against when they believe in your abilities. You're free to work on finding the best in yourself because you're not preoccupied by trying to defeat a controller. You can cooperate with someone (actually, a part of you) who wants only the best for you.

Mrs. Mellow is not the aggressive broad Mrs. Mean is. She sits back quietly and watches me fondly. To hear what she has to say, I have to consciously invite her over. Her words are balm to my troubled spirit.

"Now, honey, don't you fret about that cinnamon roll you ate last night. I'm not the least bit worried you're going to be fat. You have too much good sense to let that happen. You might gain a few pounds too much, but I know you have what it takes to lose it. I can tell you're concerned about the extra pound today. But you'll make that into something good by deciding cinnamon rolls can be enjoyed only once in awhile. See, you do use insights and awareness to help yourself become just the way you want to be! What I think is you've been pushing yourself too hard lately. Feeling stressed sometimes makes you eat unwisely. After all, you need *some* outlet, don't you? So how about if you cut back on some of your commitments? Allow some time to relax and do something fun or restful. You deserve it. You work so hard. I'm pleased you've been able to let the dust collect a few days; it doesn't matter. Visiting a friend is far more important than dusting a piano. I totally believe in your ability to decide on your priorities." And so on.

A few minutes with Mrs. Mellow leaves me smiling, content, relaxed and happy with myself. No thanks, I don't care for a cinnamon roll right now. And I don't even feel deprived!

The more you practice conjuring up this marvelous person in your life, the easier it gets. You'll feel delighted at your increased confidence as you become proficient in programming Mrs. Mellow's conversations with you.

What you tell yourself has a profound effect on your self-esteem. Filling your mind with negatives is like taking lots of small doses of poison every day. Conversely, filling your mind with positives is like taking emotional vitamins. You build your mind and spirit and make them stronger by the hour.

Some people are a bit wary of this advice. They're afraid they'll become fat, lazy slobs living in filth and squalor, being non-productive and losing jobs. On the contrary. That kind of living would make them unhappy not happy. Continuing Mrs. Mellow's kind of talk helps them reverse any destructive patterns into healthy, constructive habits. Believing in yourself makes you the best you can be!

Chapter 9

Sample Lifestyles

In this chapter, let's look at five different life goals people may have. These life goals include pleasing, charming, dependence, achieving and nurturing. We'll explore each goal, look at a sample lifestyle questionnaire and see which beliefs can be changed.

Pleasers

One of the most common problems I see in my office (and in my own life) is that of pleasing. Though everyone should be considerate and helpful, we should be as considerate and helpful to ourselves as we are to others. People who have too strong a need to please others often don't consider their own needs enough and get out of balance.

I call these people *pleasers*. Let me change that—I call *us* pleasers. Although I've made great strides in controlling my behavior, I confess to having a stronger "need" to please than I'd like to have.

Actually "need" is not quite correct. "Want" would be more appropriate. But with pleasers, the desire to please is so strong we feel it's a basic need, like food and water.

The desire to avoid disapproval colors our lives dramatically. We find ourselves agreeing to take on extra jobs or accept invitations we might prefer declining. Far too many of our decisions about how we spend our time are made with the criterion of how others will feel if we refuse.

There is an unrealistically painful fear of rejection in many of us. This formed in childhood when we truly *did* need people to take care of us and love us. We made the decision we couldn't survive without caring and love. We often live our adult lives still clinging to this irrational fear.

By adulthood, we're capable of tolerating disapproval and rejection and still enjoying full, rich, wonderful lives. But you wouldn't know it by our behavior. Watching pleasers, you'd think rejection and/or disapproval were going to assure us of an instant death.

I take comfort in meeting huge numbers of pleasers. I used to think pleasing was a rare malady suffered by only a small, unfortunate handful of overscrupulous people. I now think pleasers make up a vast army of nice guys. People find us delightful! We don't make waves. We agree. We work hard. We cooperate. We soothe, understand, give, nurture, back off and smile. What's not to like?

What's not to like is the price of that universally pleasant personality. We work so hard at pleasing that we often don't live the life we'd really like. We respect the needs of everyone else in the world but not our own. Everyone else comes first.

Sooner or later we build up resentment at the people we've tried so hard to please. We feel used and unappreciated. We may get hostile with our mates and other family members because we've accumulated a store of repressed feelings. We've "done unto others," but they haven't "done" back, at least not in the same proportion.

Sometimes the anger we experience gets shoved down deep inside and turns to depression. That's usually because we still find it almost impossible to express anger or to risk disapproval. We retreat into our "silent temper tantrum" of depression.

Of all the common maladies in the spectrum of mental nuisances, I think pleasing is the most prevalent. Pleasers fit into the world very nicely. Often we can disguise our symptoms as social interest, kindness and consideration. We're the "givers," often feeling superior to those selfish "takers" out there.

What we need is a sense of humor to help us gradually change our behavior. I look at it as a long-term plan, not something we can change overnight. We wouldn't want to do that! Society needs kindness, consideration and giving. We want to be socially interested in helping others. We just would prefer not to keep doing it for the wrong reason—an inordinate fear of disapproval.

Catching ourselves agreeing to things we'd rather not agree to is a good way to work on changing. The awareness of, "Oops, I did it again," followed by a gentle self-chuckle is healthy. It's practice. It's determining to be courageous and honest and not giving into the temptation of a quick fix. "I'll do whatever it takes for you to like me."

If we fall into that old habit 60 times this week, we can shoot for 58 times next week. Next year we may do it only 32 times a week. There's no rush. We have a lifetime to progress. The goal is to reach an awareness of our desire to please for the wrong reasons. It shows up clearly in our lifestyle. The following is a good sample of a typical pleaser.

Barbara was separated from her husband when she

came in for counseling. She admitted rather uncomfortably she enjoyed being in an apartment by herself. She loved the freedom she felt, which was mostly the absence of responsibility for others she'd carried all her life.

For a long time she'd felt put upon and controlled. She knew no other option than moving out. At last Barbara was feeling a sense of autonomy, reveling in the experience of decorating her apartment exactly as she liked without having to consider other people's desires.

When she went go back to the house she'd shared with her family, she felt squeezed, threatened and unhappy, even though her husband was trying very hard not to control her. He was determined to become respectful and loving and be the kind of husband Barbara had wanted all along. But Barbara was afraid if she moved back home, they'd fall right into the old habits of her being submissive and his being domineering.

Barbara was a classic pleaser who endured almost anything rather than risk disapproval. Seeing her beliefs in the lifestyle questionnaire helped her realize how trapped she was in her own fear of disapproval. Her unwillingness to be honest and confrontive had done as much harm to the marriage as her husband's drinking and avoidance.

After we did Barbara's lifestyle, it was obvious to her she had a lot more power than she'd realized. But she had to assert herself to be effective. She could replace her feeling of being driven to please her husband with a respectful honesty in communication. The relationship could become healthy for the first time.

Following is the lifestyle that affected Barbara's decision.

Barbara's Lifestyle Questionnaire

1. List the names and present ages of your parents and siblings in the order of their birth. Include any who died and at what age. Write three words describing each one the way you saw him when you were a child.

<u>**Name**</u>   <u>**Age**</u>   <u>**Descriptive Adjectives**</u>

Name	Age			
Dad	__	*gruff*	*intimidating*	*scared the heck out of me*
Mom	__	*kind*	*nurturing*	*accommodating*
Dan	*44*	*sweet*	*very kind*	
*Barbara	*42*	*shy*	*quiet*	*good*
Joe	*40*	*bratty*	*intelligent*	*quiet*

Middle and second child mottoes: Life is unfair. We try harder.

People should be: kind, nurturing, accommodating, sweet, intelligent, quiet and good. They shouldn't be gruff, intimidating and scare the heck out of me.

My role: shy, quiet, good.

2. Of your parents and siblings, which one was or is most like you? *Danny*

In what ways?

I am a *people-pleaser, do-gooder.*

3. Which one was most different from you? *Joe*

In what ways?

He was the smart one, who did everything well without trying.

I try hard.

4. As a small child how did you get your way?

I never got my way. I was awfully good. I pleased every-one first.

If I'm awfully good long enough and hard enough, maybe I'll get my way, but I'll accept it if I don't.

5. What kinds of compliments did you receive as a child, from parents, teachers, family, friends?

I am: *so good, such a leader, popular, teacher's pet.*

6. What kinds of negative criticism did you receive?

I am: *very skinny. "Bones."*

7. When you die (at 100, at least!) what short, descriptive phrase would you like on your tombstone to describe you as you'd *like* to be remembered?

I want to be: *a nut.*

8. If your mother had a sign over the kitchen sink to teach a strong value of hers, what would do you think it would have said?

Be good to others. Behave yourself. Be honest.

9. What would your father's sign have said?

10. What was your favorite childhood story, book or fairy tale?

Wee Woman In a Wee House

What was your favorite part of that story?

The pictures

With whom did you identify?

11. If you had to come back in another life as an animal, what would you choose to be?

Wild horse

Why?

I'd like to have no strings attached.

12. If you could wave a magic wand and change anything or anyone about your childhood, what would you change?

Dad wouldn't have used fear and gruffness to control us.

13. With that same magic wand, what or whom would you change about your life right now?

My pleasing, approval-seeking behavior.

14. What problems did you have in your childhood that you still have now?

Relationship with my father—he still intimidates me.

15. Picture the house you lived in when you were a child. Imagine yourself playing in some secluded spot by yourself. Try to remember a specific place and actually "see" yourself there right now . . . perhaps in your bedroom, in a tree, behind a bush or out in the barn. Now picture two people who were important to you then—parents, friends, grandparents; any two you want to choose.

What two people do you picture?

Mom and Grandma

Imagine you hear them talking about you, although they don't know you can hear them. Imagine their conversation. One of them says:

"She's too bossy to Margaret Mary."

The other responds:

"It bothers us to have her play so much with Margaret Mary."

What thought do you think to yourself, overhearing their remarks?

They don't know what they're talking about, the old fogies.

And what feeling (one word) do you feel?

Devastated, hurt because they didn't like me

Even if people don't know what they're talking about, I feel hurt and devastated when they disapprove of me.

Barbara's early memories

First day of school in third grade, I (worried) what I'd do all alone at recess. A girl named <u>Paula befriended me.</u> I felt (relief) because I'd been so afraid of not being accepted, having no friends, being alone.

Sitting in class watching kids eat ice cream. I felt (bad) because <u>I wanted some and didn't have money to buy any.</u> I was (mad) because I couldn't enjoy what "everyone" else was enjoying.

Trying out and <u>making cheerleader.</u> I felt so (happy) I'd "arrived" and would now be popular as a cheerleader.

I was chosen to be a soothsayer in a play. <u>Mom made me a costume. I</u> (liked) <u>having a part, but I was</u> (mad) <u>because I felt I was better than the girl who got the lead.</u>

Lee's Interpretations

I'm so afraid of not being accepted, having no friends, being alone, that I worry about it.

It's a relief to be befriended.

I feel bad and mad when I can't have what everyone else is enjoying. I have to sit and watch them.

When I "arrive" and make cheerleader, then I'll be happy!

I like being "onstage," but it's maddening not to be "center stage." (I know I'm better than whoever gets it.)

Grandpa pushed me over with his violin bow. I felt (frightened) because he disapproved of me, didn't like me.

If someone disapproves of me he might push me over with his violin bow.

During special testing in fifth grade, I felt so (frustrated) because I couldn't measure up to expectations.

Others' expectations of me frustrate me when I feel I can't measure up.

Five of us in costume sang "Beautiful Baby" and brought the principal onstage. I felt (great); I (loved) the fun and silliness.

How life should be—feeling included, "center stage," important, confident, enjoying fun and silliness.

At the blackboard in algebra, I threw an eraser back at the boy who'd thrown it a me. I was sent to the dean. I felt (sick) at being disapproved of. I had my reputation to uphold. She said, "This isn't like you."

I have a reputation to uphold—never doing anything to be disapproved of. It isn't like me.

Barbara's Beliefs
(Life is a place where . . .)

🕸 Life is unfair.

🕸 I try harder.

🕸 People should be kind, nurturing, accommodating, sweet, intelligent, quiet and good.

🕸 They shouldn't be gruff, intimidating and scare the heck out of me.

🕸 My role in life is to be shy, quiet and good. I am a people-pleaser and do-gooder.

🕸 I must try harder.

🕸 If I'm good long enough and hard enough, maybe I'll get my way, but I'll accept it if I don't.

🕸 I am so good, such a leader, popular and "teacher's pet."

🕸 I want to be a nut.

🕸 I must be good to others, behave myself and be honest.

🕸 I'm undecided whether to be a wee woman in a wee house or a wild horse with no strings attached.

🕸 I wish people wouldn't use gruffness to control me. It frightens me.

🕸 I'd like to change my pleasing, approval-seeking behavior.

🕸 My father intimidates me.

🕸 Even if people don't know what they're talking about, I feel hurt and devastated when they disapprove of me.

- I'm so afraid of not being accepted, having no friends, being alone, that I worry about it.

- It's a relief to be befriended.

- I feel bad and mad when I can't have what everyone else is enjoying. I have to sit and watch them.

- When I "arrive" and make cheerleader, <u>then</u> I'll be happy!

- I like being "onstage," but it's maddening not to be "center stage." I know I'm better than whoever gets it.

- If someone disapproves of me, he might push me over with his violin bow.

- Others' expectations of me frustrate me when I feel I can't measure up.

- How life should be—feeling included, feeling "center stage," important, confident, enjoying fun and silliness.

- I have a reputation to uphold—never doing anything to be disapproved of. It isn't like me.

Barbara's New Beliefs
(Life is a place where . . .)

- Life is unfair. *sometimes positively, sometimes negatively, to everyone.*

- I *don't have to* try harder.

- People ~~should~~ *can't always* be kind, nurturing, accommodating, sweet, intelligent, quiet and good. *and it's OK.*

- They ~~shouldn't~~ *will* be gruff, intimidating and scare the heck out of me. *but not hurt me.*

- My role in life is to be ~~shy, quiet~~ *outgoing, loud* and good, *to myself as well as others.*

- I am a *recovering* people-pleaser and do-gooder. *(Life is like diabetes; you have it forever, but with control you live a long time.)*

- I must *not* try harder.

- ~~If I'm awfully~~ *Being* good long enough and hard enough, *won't* ~~maybe I'll~~ get my way, but I'll accept it if I don't. *so I'll have to find other ways to meet my needs.*

- I ~~am~~ *don't always have to be* so good, such a leader, popular and "teacher's pet."

- I want to be a nut.

- I must be good to others, behave myself and be honest. *as long as I'm not doing it for admiration.*

- I'm ~~undecided~~ *deciding* whether ~~to~~ *I can* be a wee woman in a wee house or a wild horse with no strings attached.

- I wish people wouldn't use gruffness to control me. ~~It frightens me.~~ *I won't be manipulated by it.*

- ~~I'd like~~ *I've already begun* to change my pleasing, approval-seeking behavior.

- My father intimidates me. *only as much as I let him.*

- Even if people don't know what they're talking about, I *won't* feel hurt and devastated when they disapprove of me. *I can stand disapproval and grow from it.*

- ~~I'm so~~ *If I'm self-reliant, I'm not* afraid of not being accepted, having no friends, being alone, ~~that I worry about it.~~

- It's ~~a relief~~ *pleasant* to be befriended, *but not essential.*

- *If* I feel bad and mad when I can't have what everyone else is enjoying. ~~I have to sit and watch them.~~ *I'll find things to divert my attention.*

- When I ~~"arrive" and make cheerleader,~~ *become independent* then I'll be happy!

- I like being "onstage," but it's maddening not to be "center stage." I know I'm better than whoever gets it. *So I need to find ways to be center stage.*

- If someone disapproves of me, he might push me over with his violin bow.

🔹 Others' expectations of me frustrate me *only slightly* when I feel
   I can't measure up. *I want to measure up only to my
   own expectations.*

🔹 How life should be: feeling included, feeling "center
   stage," important, confident, enjoying fun and silliness.

🔹 I have a reputation to uphold: ~~never doing anything
   to be disapproved of. It isn't like me.~~ *doing what I
   think is right.*

Charmers

Charmers are not as prevalent as pleasers. They're like
pleasers because they loathe rejection. But they go a step
further by being able to charm their way in or out of any
situation. They're wonderful manipulators. If that sounds
negative, it has a positive side. Charmers make great sales
people, actors and public-relations executives.

A charmer is often sought after by the opposite sex.
Often he is the youngest child in the family who grew up
feeling like a prince or princess. He views the world as
here to serve him. He genuinely likes most people, and
most people like him.

Sounds marvelous, doesn't it? But there's a catch. A
charmer frequently creates such a sparkling façade the
real person inside never develops much self-esteem. He
only seems confident and "together." He inadvertently
stumbled onto the magic of act "as if" when he was a tiny
tot. It was so effective he spent his time perfecting the pre-
tense instead of improving the product.

Some charmers are like hastily constructed houses. The

wood used wasn't aged enough. Still green, it warped. The cement foundation was covered up too soon and cracked. The plaster was mixed improperly and developed weaknesses. However, it's all glitzed over with dramatic painting and special effects that take a potential homebuyer's breath away! The effect is impressive. To see the house is to love it. Only the house and the people who live in it know how imperfect it is. The weaknesses will out, regardless of how many coats of expensive stucco are applied.

The price of being a charmer is living with the need to cover up. Hiding imperfections from the world gets to be a full-time job. Despite all the efforts made, self-esteem still suffers.

But the prognosis is excellent! Charmers are bright. Once they experience the pain necessary to change themselves, they do it very effectively. Sometimes that pain is so intense they spend years dulling it with drink or drugs. Then the pain of addiction and its consequences (broken marriages, lost jobs) has to get severe enough to force the charmer to see the truth. He's *not* strong and together. He doesn't live in a castle. He's not really a prince, only a human being.

Underneath the façade is a person who's worthy and lovable in his own right. Only he must let go of the impressive costume he's worn all his life. One of the surprising benefits is how much easier life can become.

To quote my friend Anthony, "I want people to like me. I need to have their approval. I try really hard to measure up to everyone's expectations. But sometimes I work harder trying to *look* like I'm doing a good job than I would if I just did the job in the first place!"

A charmer's life is not an easy one, although it usually appears so to the rest of us. It often lacks self-discipline and is fraught with frustration caused by procrastination.

Anthony's wife said, "He is wonderful sometimes. But when he drinks, he becomes another person. He doesn't solve problems. He just tries to ignore them then gets drunk when they become too bad. All our friends think Anthony's wonderful. He can be so much fun."

Anthony said, "I don't know why I drink so much. I know I act rotten. I love my wife and my kids. I'm afraid I'm going to lose them all. I love them! I don't want to hurt them. I know I've got to quit drinking if I want to straighten out my life. I intend to quit, then I think, 'Just one more six-pack.'"

Now, several years later, Anthony is completely dry. His wife and children are delighted with him. Anthony's pleased with himself. He was wise enough to get help from several sources—counseling, AA meetings and even attendance at daily Mass. He's had several "slips" in which he tried drinking again, but he's gotten through them and back on track. His deep-down core of strength continues to build as he sees himself becoming determined, disciplined and successful.

Each time he faces a problem and confronts it, Anthony grows stronger. Using alcohol cheated him of several years of experiencing that growth. But it's easy to see how he slipped into the habit. When we see our parents avoid their problems that way, it often becomes a perfectly acceptable panacea in our own life.

Charmers and pleasers are good candidates for developing a dependency on alcohol. The harsh reality of disapproval is too painful to tolerate. Often we use alcohol or drugs to "fuzzy up the picture" and make life seem better. In doing so, we weaken rather than strengthen our courage and confidence.

Fortunately the process is reversible. Refusing to reach

for that drink is the first step.

Anthony will *always* be a charmer. But now it is a part of his personality rather than a compulsion that keeps him a prisoner of his own fears.

Following is Anthony's lifestyle questionnaire and my evaluation.

Anthony's Lifestyle Questionnaire

1. List the names and present ages of your parents and siblings in the order of their birth. Include any who died and at what age. Write three words describing each one the way you saw him when you were a child.

Name	Age	Descriptive Adjectives		
Dad	__	strong foundation	epitome of manhood	religious and alcoholic
Mom	__	lazy, sickly	dependable	alcoholic (died of it)
Mark	45	strong	trouble	fighting
Lorraine	41	dependable	replacement	for mother
Karen	36	happy	sound	feminine
John	34	"old brother"	respectful	my idol
Brad	33	my partner	my friend	companion
*Anthony	31	chosen	a leader	athlete

Youngest's motto: I'm entitled.

I had a lot of people to depend on—strong foundation, epitome of manhood, dependable, strong, dependable, replacement for mother, sound, older brother, respectful, my idol, my partner, my friend, companion.

I'm special. Alcoholics solve problems by running from them.

2. Of your parents and siblings, which one was or is most like you? *Mark*

In what ways?

We always got our way. (Later both of us abused drugs.)

3. Which one was most different from you? *Brad*

In what ways?

He doesn't seem to have problems applying himself like I do.

4. As a small child how did you go about getting your way?

I'd do whatever was necessary to please people; make it look like I'm doing it but do whatever I want; be a brown-nose.

5. What kinds of compliments did you receive as a child, from parents, teachers, family, friends?

I was always elected to lead the pack.

6. What kinds of negative criticism did you receive?

Not very smart, damn dummy (Dad), you should be reading. My weight.

7. When you die (at 100, at least!) what short, descriptive phrase would you like on your tombstone to describe you as you'd *like* to be remembered?

"Lived for 31 years and finally got it together."

8. If your mother had a sign over the kitchen sink to teach a strong value of hers, what would it have said?

"Get the grades."

9. What would your father's sign have said?

"Education is important."

10. What was your favorite childhood story, book or fairy tale?

I had an erotic fantasy for Betty Boop.
What was your favorite part of that story?
With whom did you identify?
11. If you had to come back in another life as an animal, what would you choose to be? *Bird*
Why?
Freedom—able to fly whenever I want.
(I don't want to <u>have</u> to do anything.)
12. If you could wave a magic wand and change anything or anyone about your childhood, what would you change?
For Dad to be more open and able to convey a sincere response of love.
(I didn't learn how to be open and loving.)
13. With that same magic wand, what or whom would you change about your life right now?
Myself—to be disciplined.
14. What problems did you have in your childhood that you still have now?
Self-discipline and a denial game. I won't deal with situations. I'm very shallow in evaluation of myself and others.
15. Picture the house you lived in when you were a child. Imagine yourself playing in some secluded spot by yourself. Try to remember a specific place and actually "see" yourself there right now . . . perhaps in your bedroom, in a tree, behind a bush or out in the barn. Now picture two people who were important to you then—parents, friends, grandparents; any two you want to choose. What two people do you picture?
    Lorraine and Dad
Imagine you hear them talking about you, although they don't know you can hear them. Imagine their conversation. One of them says:

Lorraine says, "He's cute."
The other responds:
Dad says, "A good boy."
What thought do you think to yourself, overhearing their remarks?
Not really so. They don't really know the real me. I don't think I'm as good as others think I am.
And what feeling (one word) do you feel?
Sad.

Anthony's Early Memories	**Lee's Interpretations**
My pant leg caught in a bike chain. <u>I had to take them off in front of some girls and my brother.</u> I didn't want anyone to see how fat I was. My brother was saying it was OK. I felt embarrassed and mortified.	I shouldn't be imperfect in any way. If I am, no one should find out about it. People should comfort me and reassure me.
I wet my bed. I hated the odor as <u>I sat there waiting to be changed.</u> I felt choked and guilty that I'd done it. I felt disgust from the person who changed me.	If I make a mistake, I'm disgusted, and I feel guilty. People need to take care of me.

I ran into a screen door. <u>Everyone was telling me it wasn't that bad.</u> I felt (frightened.)

I was carrying chlorine into a house. A dog came and jumped on me. I fell back. The bottle broke. Chlorine got all over me. <u>I had to go to a hospital.</u> I was (scared) I'd lose my eyesight. <u>They were saying the chlorine was eating through my clothes.</u> I felt (fearful) and (bad) that I'd ruined the visit to Knott's Berry Farm.

We were all in the car. Dad was drunk but fun. He drove behind a car and "teased" the other driver. They had a fight at a stop sign. <u>Mom and Dad fought. He left.</u> She called to him, but he kept walking. I felt (concern) and (astonishment.)

Dad was helping me with math. He'd say, "Damn, you stupid son of a bitch! What the hell is wrong with you?" <u>He'd hit me.</u> I felt (sad.)

If I hurt myself, people will rush to rescue and comfort me, especially if I'm frightened.

If I make mistakes, bad things will happen to me.

I'm responsible for other people's disappointments.

When you're drunk, you can act superior and be fun.

I'm concerned and astonished at the thought of having someone I love <u>leave</u> me.

If I make mistakes I'm bad and stupid and need to be punished.

I feel sad that there's some-

I'd cry and say I'd tell Mom. I'd break away and go to Mom, lay my head on her and cry. I felt (like a failure) because I wanted to please him.

thing wrong with me; I'm a failure.

On her deathbed, Mom told Dad to be good to me. That was a green light.

People should be good to me.

I should be allowed to do whatever I want to do.

Anthony's Beliefs
(Life is a place where . . .)

- I'm entitled.
- Strength and dependability are family values.
- You solve problems by running from them.
- I'm special, chosen, a leader.
- I should always get my way and do what I want.
- I have trouble applying myself.
- I can make it <u>look</u> like I'm doing something, but do what I want.
- I'm popular, respected and can lead the pack.
- I am finally getting it together.
- Education is important.
- I don't want to <u>have</u> to do anything.
- I don't know how to be open and loving.

- I would like to be more disciplined.

- I don't think I'm as good as others think I am.

- I shouldn't be imperfect in any way; if I am, no one should find out about it.

- People should comfort me and reassure me.

- If I make a mistake, I'm disgusting and I feel guilty.

- People need to take care of me.

- If I hurt myself, people will rush to rescue and comfort me, especially if I'm frightened.

- If I make mistakes, bad things will happen to me.

- I'm responsible for other people's disappointments.

- When you're drunk, you can act superior and be fun.

- I'm concerned and astonished at the thought of having someone I love <u>leave</u> me.

- If I make mistakes, I'm bad and stupid and need to be punished.

- I feel sad that there's something wrong with me; I'm a failure.

- I want someone to comfort me.

- People should be good to me.

- I should be allowed to do whatever I want to do.

Anthony's New Beliefs
(Life is a place where . . .)

- I'm *not* entitled. *to everything I want.*

- Strength and dependability are family values. *but perfection is bad.*

- You solve problems by ~~running from~~ *facing and tackling* them.

- I'm special, chosen, a leader.

- ~~I~~ *Nobody* should always get ~~my~~ *his* way and do what ~~I~~ *he* want*s*.

- I have trouble applying myself. *but I'm happiest when I do it.*

- I can make it <u>look</u> like I'm doing something but do what I want. *but I might as well do it.*

- I'm popular, respected and can lead the pack.

- I am finally getting it together.

- Education is important.

- I don't want to <u>have</u> to do anything. *but that's part of life.*

- I ~~don't~~ know how to be open and loving. *by telling my feelings respectfully.*

- I would like to be more disciplined. *and I've made a good start.*

- I don't think I'm as good *or as bad* as others think I am.

- ~~I shouldn't be imperfect in any way, or if I am no one should find out about it.~~ *It's OK to be imperfect.*

🐾 People should comfort me and reassure me. *and they may if I ask.*

🐾 If I make a mistake, ~~I'm disgusting and I feel guilty.~~ *I can learn from it, confess it and let guilt go.*

🐾 People need to take care of ~~me.~~ *themselves and each other.*

🐾 If I hurt myself, people ~~will~~ *won't* rush to rescue and comfort me, ~~especially if I'm frightened.~~ *and that's OK.*

🐾 If I make mistakes, ~~bad things will happen to me.~~ *I can learn from them*

🐾 I'm *not necessarily* responsible for other people's disappointments.

🐾 ~~When you're drunk, you can act superior and be fun.~~

🐾 I'm concerned and astonished at the thought of having someone I love <u>leave</u> me.

🐾 If ~~I~~ *people* make mistakes, ~~I'm~~ *they aren't* bad and stupid and *don't* need to be punished.

🐾 ~~I feel sad~~ *It's not true* that there's something wrong with me; I'm *not* a failure.

🐾 I want someone to comfort me. *and someone may if I ask.*

🐾 People should be good to me. *if I deserve it.*

🐾 ~~I~~ *Nobody* should be allowed to do whatever ~~I~~ *they* want to do.

Dependers

Dependency is the worst position in which you might find yourself. A *dependent* person decides in childhood his life is in the hands of others. He struggles to get his family to notice him, like him, include him, admire him and make his life happy. Much of the time he fails.

A dependent person feels miserable in the face of rejection. She chalks it up to proof that her happiness depends on the actions of those she wants to like her. She tries even harder. She pulls every trick in the book to win people over. She works relentlessly to manipulate them.

If being sweet and charming seems to bring the best results, she'll be sweet and charming. If sickness works best, she'll be sick. If temper tantrums make people sit up and take notice, she'll polish her tantrum skills. Her aim is to get people to pay attention to her and make her feel important. If she has to suffer to do it, she'll suffer.

Rebecca came to me as a depressed young woman. She felt unloved and unwanted. She was so depressed she rarely even made eye contact with me. Mostly she looked down at her lap. She had no boyfriends. The girlfriends she had often disappointed her.

Her family seemed not to care much about her and made her feel excluded. She had a sadness about her that made her look uninteresting. She wasn't the object of flirtation when she went to a party or a singles' bar. She was the picture of depression.

Depression is a "silent" temper tantrum. Counseling often begins with discovering the cause for the anger, which may be unrecognized or denied. The next step, doing the lifestyle questionnaire, helps find the mistaken beliefs the person formed in childhood.

When Rebecca was ignored or not included as a little

girl, she "sat down mad." Becoming inactive and non-involved often got results. Someone was forced to attend to her if she looked sufficiently sad. It was natural for Rebecca to continue believing in her "neediness." She got depressed and would "sit down mad" whenever she felt shut out or unappreciated.

But as an adult, she found it harder to get others to feel sorry for her and come to her rescue. When she acted depressed and down, she frequently turned people off. Nobody wanted to be around a "downer," so Rebecca felt even more rejected. She tried harder to look sad and needy, waiting for somebody to seek her out.

This process is a vicious cycle of discouragement. The person must realize acting sad keeps people at bay instead of creating closeness.

Rebecca has an inordinate thirst for self-improvement. She sought counseling from many sources, including religious leaders, psychics and tarot-card readers. Over her 6-year counseling period, she got a degree in nursing, had several boyfriends and met the man she's marrying.

I think the way she met her future husband is delightful. He was one of many who answered her ad in a singles' magazine. The chemistry was right. How wonderfully aggressive that kind of behavior is when you realize Rebecca was once the little girl who thought she had to sit down and be mad if no one would play with her.

Rebecca's Lifestyle Questionnaire

1. List the names and present ages of your parents and siblings in the order of their birth. Include any who died and at what age. Write three words describing each one the way you saw him when you were a child.

Name	Age	Descriptive Adjectives		
Dad	—	*loving*	*big*	*fun*
Mom	—	*authority*	*busy*	*beautiful*
P*aul*	*30*	*protective*	*big*	*loving*
Linda	*26*	*independent*	*friendly*	*strong*
Sue	*23*	*exciting*	*independent*	*strong*
*Rebecca	*20*	*good*	*shy, quiet*	*tag-along*

Youngest's motto: I'm entitled.

Other people are—loving, big, fun, authorities, busy, beautiful, protective, independent, friendly, strong, exciting.

I am the good shy, quiet tag-along.

I must depend on others.

2. Of your parents and siblings, which one was or is most like you?

None

In what ways?

3. Which one was most different from you?

Sue

In what ways?

I'm not: *independent, never scared to try anything, very social*.

4. As a small child how did you go about getting your way?

I should get my way *by being good and saying "please."*

5. What kinds of compliments did you receive as a child, from parents, teachers, family, friends?

I should be *a good girl*.

6. What kinds of negative criticism did you receive?

You're bad. I should be bad (disobey, take risks).

7. When you die (at 100, at least!) what short, descriptive phrase would you like on your tombstone to describe you as you'd *like* to be remembered?

I want to be *"loving and caring."*

8. If your mother had a sign over the kitchen sink to teach a strong value, what would it have said?

"Honesty." I want to be honest.

9. What would your father's sign have said?

"Honesty."

10. What was your favorite childhood story, book or fairy tale?

Invincible Louisa.

What was your favorite part of that story?

She was very active and always getting into things.

With whom did you identify?

Louisa. I wished I were like her. I wish I could be active and into things.

11. If you had to come back in another life as an animal, what would you choose to be?

Cat

Why?

I want to be *independent, loving, know what they want, soft, strong*.

12. If you could wave a magic wand and change anything or anyone about your childhood, what would you change?

Parents not so scared of everything.

13. With that same magic wand, what or whom would you change about your life right now?

Parents would be younger and not so critical of others.

14. What problems did you have in your childhood that you still have now?

15. Picture the house you lived in when you were a child. Imagine yourself playing in some secluded spot by yourself. Try to remember a specific place and actually "see" yourself there right now . . . perhaps in your bedroom, in a tree, behind a bush or out in the barn. Now picture two people who were important to you then—parents, friends, grandparents; any two you want to choose. What two people do you picture?

Sue and cousin

Imagine you hear them talking about you, although they don't know you can hear them. Imagine their conversation. One of them says:

Cousin says, "Good, we got rid of her."

The other responds:

Sue says, "She's not so bad."

What thought do you think to yourself, overhearing their remarks?

"They don't like me." Even if someone defends me I'll still believe they don't like me.

And what feeling (one word) do you feel?

Hurt, rejection hurts.

Rebecca's Early Memories

<u>Waiting on the steps</u> for Dad to come home. When he did, I ran into his arms. He picked me up, swung me and hugged me. It was (great.) Best part of the day. Then I played around while he read the paper. Waiting was (exciting.)

I'd been sick. Mom said, "Don't go out and play." I said OK, and she left. Gracie came over and wanted to show me a neat house. I went and had a (great) time. I came back, and Mom was there. She said, "You know you did wrong. I've got to spank you." She did. <u>Right before she spanked me</u> I felt (scared.)

I'd fought with someone so no one would let me play with them. As I was riding my bike, a branch went into my leg. I screamed bloody murder. I <u>stood there crying,</u> feeling (angry) and (lonely.) People came out, helped me into the car,

Lee's Interpretations

I'm still waiting on the steps for someone to come home, pick me up, swing me and hug me.

If I take a risk and go do something fun, I'll get hurt for it. That's scary.

If I hurt myself and scream bloody murder, people will come to my rescue. Then I won't have to be angry and lonely.

took me home. My cousins took me to the hospital, but they couldn't sew up my leg till Mom came. Mom finally came.

It was Easter. I was dressed up and playing with Joanie. Aunt Minnie yelled at us, "What are you doing out there without your shoes on?" I was scared to death of her, frozen in my tracks. "I have my shoes on," I said. She said, "OK."

When I'm scared to death, I'm frozen in my tracks.

I was at the beach with my sisters and cousins. They got ahead of me. I yelled at them, "Wait for me, wait for me!" They wouldn't. I sat down mad. They came back. I knew they'd get in trouble. I was really mad.

When people won't wait for me or include me, I'll sit down mad. Then they'll come back, and they'll get in trouble.

I went to the Polo Club for a swimming lesson. When I found the teacher was a man, I got scared and nervous. I sat on the edge of the pool and cried and wouldn't go in with him.

If I'm scared and nervous, I'll sit on the edge of the pool and cry and not go in the water.

Joanie and I took a bath. I fell on the tub rail and cried and <u>cried and wouldn't stop.</u> They had to take me home. I wasn't scared right then, but Aunt Minnie wasn't sympathetic and soothing about my pain. Mom took care of me when I was hurt. I felt mad.

When I cry and cry and won't stop, someone will have to take care of me.

People should be sympathetic and soothing about my pain if I get hurt.

Rebecca's Beliefs
(Life is a place where . . .)

- I'm entitled.
- Other people are loving, big, fun, authorities, busy, beautiful, protective, independent, friendly, strong, exciting.
- I am the good, shy, quiet tag-along. I must depend on others.
- I'm not independent. I'm scared to try anything. I'm not social.
- If I'm good and say "please," I should get my way.
- I should always be good. I shouldn't be bad (disobey, take risks).
- I want to be loving, caring and honest.
- I wish I could be more active and into things, but I'm not.

- I want to be independent, loving, soft, strong and know what I want.

- Even if someone defends me, I'll believe they don't like me.

- Rejection hurts.

- I'm still waiting on the steps for someone to come home, pick me up, swing me and hug me. Waiting is exciting.

- If I take a risk and go do something fun, I'll get hurt for it.

- If I hurt myself and scream bloody murder, people will come to my rescue. Then I won't have to be angry and lonely.

- When I'm scared to death, I freeze in my tracks.

- When people won't wait for me or include me, I'll sit down mad.

- If I'm scared and nervous, I'll sit on the edge of the pool and cry and not go in the water.

- When I cry and won't stop, someone will have to take care of me.

- People should be sympathetic and soothing about my pain if I get hurt.

Rebecca's New Beliefs
(Life is a place where . . .)

- I'm entitled.

- Other people are loving, big, fun, authorities, busy, beautiful, protective, independent, friendly, strong, exciting. *I can be, too.*

- I am ~~the good, shy, quiet tagalong.~~ *respectful, assertive and confident* I must depend on ~~others.~~ *myself.*

- I'm not independent. I'm *not* scared to try anything. I'm not social.

- *Even* If I'm good and say "please," I ~~should~~ *may not always* get my way. *I will discuss and negotiate respectfully.*

- I should always be ~~good.~~ *respectful, but if I slip I'm still OK.* I shouldn't be bad (disobey, take risks). *but everyone makes mistakes. I'll forgive myself and others for them.*

- I want to be loving, caring and honest.

- I ~~wish I could~~ *can* be more active and into things, ~~but I'm not.~~ *and I will.*

- I want to be independent, loving, soft, strong and know what I want.

- *When* ~~Even if~~ someone defends me, I'll believe they ~~don't~~ like me. *or at least respect me.*

- Rejection hurts. *but I can stand it. Practice makes it easier.*

- *Rather than* ~~I'm still~~ waiting on the steps for someone to come home, pick me up, swing me and hug me. *I think I'll go do something I'd enjoy doing!*

- If I take a risk and go do something fun, I'll ~~get hurt for it.~~ *probably have a good time.*

I don't have to stay angry and lonely if I make myself happy alone or with others.

ᴥ ~~If I hurt myself and scream bloody murder, people will come to my rescue, and then I won't have to be angry and lonely.~~

                 I'll move my muscles and take action.
ᴥ When I'm scared to death, ~~freeze in my tracks.~~

ᴥ When people won't wait for me or include me, I'll ~~sit down mad.~~ *find an activity I can enjoy alone or with others.*

ᴥ When I cry and won't stop ~~someone will have to take care of me.~~ *I'll exhaust myself. I can decide to change my activity, my thoughts, my feelings.*

      won't always
ᴥ People ~~should~~ be sympathetic and soothing about my pain if I get hurt.

Achievers

People with a strong priority to achieve usually believe they are worthwhile only when they are achieving. Once they accomplish something, they quickly cast about for something else to achieve. The process never ends. These people can easily become the Type-A personalities medical journals warn us about. Achievers are driven to succeed and accomplish more than is healthy for them.

You could probably spot potential achievers in kindergarten. The little boy who was the apple of the teacher's eye did his work correctly and efficiently. He may have sharpened his skills into adulthood. The little girl who volunteered to clean the fish tank after she whipped through the "color the gingerbread house" exercise was a budding young achiever.

Achievers find it hard to enjoy sitting and watching TV. They prefer to get the ironing done, polish their shoes or brush the dog while they watch. Doing two or three things at once is bliss to the hard-core achiever. Vacations can be hell, unless they tour the entire island and see all the tourist attractions before going to another spot to repeat the process.

Achievers may not attend to their relationships because they're too busy. If two achievers marry, they may rarely see each other. They're both filled with important activities.

If they live in nursing homes in their golden years, achievers still do many things. They may contribute heavily to the home's weekly newspaper, stack the bingo cards, head the hospitality committee, remind the directors of Valentine's Day and help keep track of Emma's dentures.

An achiever's complaints are usually due to overextension of some kind. He may long for a few days off, only to discover he fills his days off cleaning out the garage and starting a vegetable garden.

Claude, a typical achiever, was a reluctant partner in marriage counseling. He was there only because his wife was going to file for divorce if he didn't come. He seemed to be the ideal husband—handsome, extremely successful in business, well-known around town. He was generous with his wife and children. But he had one flaw: no time for them.

Claude saw absolutely nothing wrong with his life except his wife's complaints. "I think Karen is unrealistic in her demands," he said. "The reason I spend so much time at my job is to be able to give her and the children all the things they want. Yet she's always mad I'm not home with them more." He was genuinely puzzled as to how Karen could criticize him. He had learned as a child hard work should bring praise and rewards.

Fortunately, Claude is smart and able to achieve whatever he goes after. It was just a matter of seeing his tunnel-vision approach to life left no room for a close, intimate relationship. His determination to succeed was impressive. Once he recognized what was missing, there was no doubt in his or anyone else's mind he would succeed in this challenge.

Claude began buying self-help books that taught communication skills. He invested in audio tapes for his car that explained women and relationships. He pencilled off free hours in his appointment book for doing things with his family.

Karen now has plenty of opportunity to praise Claude. She rewards him for the progress he's made in changing his lifestyle to include her and the children. Both of us encouraged the tenacity he showed in setting goals and achieving them. He polished his romantic skills with the same determination he once used learning to swim. Once again he could say, "I got to surprise everyone and show I could do it!"

Following is Claude's lifestyle questionnaire and my interpretations.

Claude's Lifestyle Questionnaire

1. List the names and present ages of your parents and siblings in the order of their birth. Include any who died and at what age. Write three words describing each one the way you saw him when you were a child.

<u>**Name**</u> <u>**Age**</u> <u>**Descriptive Adjectives**</u>

<u>**Dad**</u> _ _busy_ _stern_ _important_

<u>**Mom**</u> _ _loving_ _friendly_ _happy_

*_Claude_ _40_ (_smart_ _well-liked_ _funny_)

Melinda _37_ _spoiled_ _artistic_ _selfish_

Oldest's motto: (I was here first, and first I'll stay.)

(People should be busy, important, loving, friendly, happy, smart, well-liked, funny and artistic, not stern, spoiled and selfish.)

(I'm smart, well-liked and funny.)

2. Of your parents and siblings, which one was or is most like you?

Dad

In what ways?

(I am _always busy doing things._)

3. Which one was most different from you?

Melinda

In what ways?

(I don't _need to be taken care of._)

4. As a small child how did you go about getting your way?

(_Asked, used reason, argued relentlessly._)

5. What kinds of compliments did you receive as a child, from parents, teachers, family, friends?

(I am *smart, good.*)

6. What kinds of negative criticism did you receive?

7. When you die (at 100, at least!) what short, descriptive phrase would you like on your tombstone to describe you as you'd *like* to be remembered?

(*He succeeded at everything he tried.*)

8. If your mother had a sign over the kitchen sink to teach a strong value of hers, what would it have said?

(*"Get good grades!"*)

9. What would your father's sign have said?

(*"Do it right!"*)

10. What was your favorite childhood story, book or fairy tale?

    Little Engine That Could

What was your favorite part of that story?

(*He did what he wanted to do.*)

With whom did you identify?

    Engine.

11. If you had to come back in another life as an animal, what would you choose to be?

    Beaver.

Why?

(I am *project-oriented, hard-working.*)

12. If you could wave a magic wand and change anything or anyone about your childhood, what would you change?

    I'd have been *taller sooner and better at sports.*

13. With that same magic wand, what or whom would you change about your life right now?

    Have our marriage run more smoothly.

14. What problems did you have in your childhood that you still have now?

(*Fear of disapproval*)

15. Picture the house you lived in when you were a child. Imagine yourself playing in some secluded spot by yourself. Try to remember a specific place and actually "see" yourself there right now . . . perhaps in your bedroom, in a tree, behind a bush or out in the barn. Imagine yourself where you used to be as a child. Now picture two people who were important to you then— parents, friends, grandparents; any two you want to choose.

What two people do you picture?

Mom and Dad

Imagine you hear them talking about you, although they don't know you can hear them. Imagine their conversation. One of them says:

"Claude brought home straight A's again."

The other responds:

"He's going to amount to something."

What thought do you think to yourself, overhearing their remarks?

I'll work hard and amount to something.

And what feeling (one word) do you feel?

Happy.

Claude's Early Memories

I got a red fire engine with pedals. Dad lifted me in, and I figured out how to pedal to make it go. Every-one stood on the sidewalk and raved about how smart I was. I felt proud.

Lee's Interpretations

I'm proud when I figure out how to do something and everyone is impressed with me.

I went to a birthday party. We played a game where you had to find as many words in "Happy Birthday" as you could. <u>I won and got a prize.</u> I felt (thrilled.)

It's thrilling to be the best and win recognition for it.

My friend and I were the last two still going in an all-school spelling bee. My parents and grandparents were in the audience. I didn't know how to spell "psychological," and he won. <u>Seeing the disappointment on my father's face</u> was (horrible.) I felt agony at having failed.

To make a mistake is to feel agony.

It's horrible to disappoint people who depend on me to succeed.

I went with my father to his office one Saturday morning. <u>Everyone spoke to him.</u> I was (impressed;) he was so well-known and important then.

I must never fail.

Being well-known and important is a big value to me.

My little sister learned to swim before I did. <u>I hated it that she could do something I couldn't.</u> I felt (angry) and (resentful.) So, every day after school, I went secretly to a friend's house who had a pool. I was determined to learn to swim,

I hate having someone be better than I.

Feeling second-class makes me angry and resentful.

I achieve whatever I set out to.

and I did it. I got to surprise everyone and show I could do it. I felt (ecstatic) at no longer being "Number Two."

I'm determined to reach my goal, and I'm ecstatic when I succeed.

Mr. Keller hired me to clean his drugstore one summer. I worked hard at it and felt so (proud.) He complimented me on how shiny the soda fountain was. I was so (glad) he noticed it!

Working hard and feeling proud of it is important to me.

I'm so glad when someone recognizes my effort with a pat on the back.

Claude's Beliefs
(Life is a place where . . .)

- I was here first, and first I'll stay.
- People should be busy, important, friendly, happy, smart, well-liked, funny and artistic, not stern, spoiled and selfish.
- I'm smart, well-liked and funny.
- I must always be busy doing things.
- I don't need to be taken care of.
- I have many ways of getting my needs met—asking, reasoning, arguing relentlessly.
- I must always be smart and good.
- I will succeed at everything I try.
- I will "get good grades" (do a good job at my work).
- Do it right!

- I want to be able to do what I want to do.
- I am project-oriented and hard-working.
- I want my marriage to run more smoothly.
- I fear disapproval.
- I work hard to amount to something.
- I'm proud when I figure out how to do something and everyone is impressed with me.
- It's thrilling to be best and win recognition for it.
- To make a mistake is to feel agony.
- It's horrible to disappoint people who depend on me to succeed.
- I must never fail.
- Being well-known and important is a big value to me.
- I hate having someone be better than I.
- Feeling second class makes me angry and resentful.
- I achieve whatever I set out to do.
- I'm determined to reach my goal, and I'm ecstatic when I succeed.
- Working hard and feeling proud of it is important to me.
- I'm so glad when someone recognizes my efforts with a pat on the back.

Claude's New Beliefs
(Life is a place where . . .)

- I was here first, ~~and first I'll stay.~~ *but I don't have to be first always.*

- *I want to balance work and pleasure.*
  ~~People should be busy, important, friendly, happy, smart, well-liked, funny and artistic . . . not stern, spoiled and selfish.~~

- I'm smart, well-liked and funny.

-   *like to*
  I ~~must always~~ be busy doing things. *and I like playing or relaxing.*

- I don't need to be taken care of.

- I have many ways of getting my needs met—asking, reasoning, arguing relentlessly.

- I must always be smart and good.

-   *don't have to*
  I ~~will~~ succeed at everything I try.

- I will "get good grades" (do a good job at my work). *and also in my marriage.*

- Do it right!

- I want to be able to do what I want to do. *but I must consider others' needs as well.*

- I am project-oriented and hard-working.

- I want my marriage to run more smoothly. *and I know I can achieve <u>that</u> goal.*

- I fear disapproval. *but I can learn and grow from it.*

- I work hard to amount to something.

- I'm proud when I figure out how to do something and everyone is impressed with me.

- It's thrilling to be best and win recognition for it. *but I want to be happy when I'm not competing, too.*

- To make a mistake is ~~to feel agony~~. *OK.*

- It's ~~horrible~~ *uncomfortable* to disappoint people who depend on me to succeed.

- ~~I must never fail~~. *It's OK to fail if I learn something from it.*

- Being well-known and important is a big value to me. *So is loving.*

- I hate having someone be better than I. *but I can't be best at everything.*

- Feeling second class makes me angry and resentful. *but no one can be best at everything.*

- I *usually* achieve whatever I set out to do.

- I'm determined to reach my goal, and I'm ecstatic when I succeed.

- Working hard and feeling proud of it is important to me.

- I'm so glad when someone recognizes my efforts with a pat on the back.

Nurturers

Millie is a typical nurturer. She is one of the dearest women you could ever meet. At 79 she was referred to me for counseling by her doctor because of some stomach problems he attributed to stress.

Formerly a social worker, Millie was still actively involved helping many people in her life. Still in love with her husband of 41 years, she nurtured him with enthusiasm.

"I get up at 7:00 to get him a good breakfast," she twinkled. "I fix him a good lunch and a good dinner, too." She also wrote her sister a "nice, long letter" every week in addition to helping this friend and that neighbor. There was not a bit of self-pity in her manner. I could tell she enjoyed each of the people she was involved with.

Millie was the epitome of what we call *social interest*. This is Alfred Adler's term for caring about our fellow man. People with a lot of social interest are almost always happy people. Caring for others seems to help keep them filled with zest for life. Millie beamed as she told me about the child to whom she teaches piano. She said how grateful she was to his parents for taking her to the symphony with them because she can't drive at night. Clearly she thrived on her busy involvement with many people.

Then where was the stress coming from?

Millie didn't allow time for *herself*. She confessed to wishing she could just go off by herself to read for an hour or two. But her schedule didn't have any spare hours.

Couldn't she let go of some of her nurturing for others and nurture herself? Of course she could. But she wasn't aware of how much she hungered for that occasional solitude. Her stomach was trying to tell her something was out of balance.

Millie's husband was also very much in love with her. He was more than happy to cooperate in any way he could. All Millie needed was to get over her feeling of guilt if she did something she wanted to do for herself. Somehow she had come to believe as a child you must help people, even if you don't feel like it.

Seeing her beliefs at the end of the lifestyle questionnaire helped Millie realize she was not respecting her own needs. She became conscientious about doing her "homework" of spending time nurturing herself. After only four sessions, her doctor released her. All she had needed was a little self-nurturing.

Millie's Lifestyle Questionnaire

1. List the names and present ages of your parents and siblings in the order of their birth. Include any who died and at what age. Write three words describing each one the way you saw him when you were a child.

Name	Age	Descriptive Adjectives		
				helping
Dad	_	*hardworking*	*honest, loving people*	
			very	*loving, doing*
Mom	_	*very devoted*	*dependable*	*for others*
		thoughtful	*kind,*	*worked hard,*
Reg	_	*of others*	*easygoing*	*did well*
			I worshipped	*talented*
Lonnie	_	*very capable*	*her*	*musically*
			very	*do my part*
*Millie	_	*happy*	*responsible*	*of the work*

People should be hardworking, honest, loving, help people, very devoted, very dependable, do for others, thoughtful of others, kind, work hard, do well, capable. I am happy, very responsible to do my part of the work.
2. Of your parents and siblings, which one was or is most like you?

Dad

In what ways?

I am *interested in other people*.

3. Which one was most different from you?

Lonnie

In what ways?

I'm not *a manipulator*.

4. As a small child how did you get your way?

Crawled up on Father's lap, kissed and hugged him.

Being affectionate and loving is the best way to get my needs met.

5. What kinds of compliments did you receive as a child, from parents, teachers, family, friends?

Did well in school—one of the top two in the class.

I am smart and conscientious.

6. What kinds of negative criticism did you receive?

7. When you die (at 100, at least!) what short, descriptive phrase would you like on your tombstone to describe you as you'd *like* to be remembered?

She cared about others.

8. If your mother had a sign over the kitchen sink to teach a strong value of hers, what would it have said?

"Love."

9. What would your father's sign have said?

"Love."

10. What was your favorite childhood story, book or fairy tale?

The Bobbsey Twins

What was your favorite part of that story?

What they did

With whom did you identify?

11. If you had to come back in another life as an animal, what would you choose to be?

Cat.

Why?

I'd like to be soft and beautiful and very spoiled, well taken care of.

12. If you could wave a magic wand and change anything or anyone about your childhood, what would you change?

I'd have been allowed to dance. (My parents didn't believe it was right.)

13. With that same magic wand, what or whom would you change about your life right now?

I'd be strong and healthy.

14. What problems did you have in your childhood that you still have now?

Never strong—stomach upsets.

15. Picture the house you lived in when you were a child. Imagine yourself playing in some secluded spot by yourself. Try to remember a specific place and actually "see" yourself there right now . . . perhaps in your bedroom, in a tree, behind a bush or out in the barn. Now picture two people who were important to you then—parents, friends, grandparents; any two you want to choose. What two people do you picture?

Mother and Father

Imagine you hear them talking about you, although they don't know you can hear them. Imagine their conversation. One of them says:

Mother said, "Millie wants to go back to the woods to play."

The other responds:

"She said she'd bring my lunch to me."

Then Mother said,

"I'll bring it to you."

What thought do you think to yourself, overhearing their remarks?

I felt guilty that Mother had to go, but I wanted to go play.

And what feeling (one word) do you feel?

Confused. I'm torn between my obligation to do for others and my desire to enjoy myself.

Millie's Early Memories

Mother and I walked down the road to meet my father, brother and sister. They didn't get to the bridge. We went home and found them there. I felt happy enjoying the scenery but a little upset they didn't come.

My best memory is the love and joy in our home—the family togetherness.

We were playing in the playground, and my friend Alice fell out of the swing. I felt so bad.

I was standing over a heat register, having a good time. It was fun.

I was watching people dance. Frances tried to teach me. I felt guilty; I didn't want my parents to know.

Lee's Interpretations

I'm happy doing pleasant things with someone I love.

It's upsetting when people don't fulfill my expectations.

Life should be a home filled with love, joy and family togetherness.

I feel bad when anyone else is hurt.

I love having a good time and fun.

I feel guilty when I'm having fun someone else would disapprove of.

Dad got upset when Reg spent too much money. That upset me. Mom would try to calm Dad, to make him feel better.

I get upset when others are upset.

Women should try to calm men and make them feel better.

My grandparents were coming for Christmas. We had to wait for them and my brother before we could celebrate. I felt impatient and a little angry. I went to my room and looked out the window.

Having to wait for joy and celebration makes me impatient and a little angry.

I handle it best by going to my room and looking out the window.

Mom took me with her to visit poor families to help them. She impressed on me they were as good as we were, only poor. I felt a little above some of them. I didn't like the conditions, but knew I had to go.

You should help people even if you don't feel like it.

Millie's Beliefs
(Life is a place where . . .)

- People should be hardworking, honest, loving, helping people, very devoted, very dependable, doing for others, thoughtful of others, kind, doing well and capable.

- I am happy, very responsible and do my part of the work.

- ▰ I am interested in other people.
- ▰ I'm not a manipulator of people
- ▰ Being affectionate and loving is the best way to go about getting my needs met.
- ▰ I'm smart and conscientious.
- ▰ I care about others.
- ▰ If you love, you do what others want you to do.
- ▰ I want to be allowed to do what I want to do.
- ▰ It would be nice to be soft and beautiful, very spoiled and well taken care of.
- ▰ I'm torn between my obligation to do for others and my desire to enjoy myself.
- ▰ I'm happy doing pleasant things with someone I love.
- ▰ It's upsetting when people don't fulfill my expectations.
- ▰ Life should be a home filled with love, joy and family togetherness.
- ▰ I feel bad when anyone else is hurt.
- ▰ I love having a good time and fun.
- ▰ I feel guilty when I'm having fun someone else would disapprove of.
- ▰ I get upset when others are upset.
- ▰ Women should try to calm men and make them feel better.
- ▰ Having to wait for joy and celebration makes me impatient and a little angry.

🍃 I handle frustration best by going alone to my room and looking out the window.

🍃 You should help people even if you don't feel like it.

Millie's New Beliefs
(Life is a place where . . .)

🍃 People ~~should~~ *can't always* be hardworking, honest, loving, helping, very devoted, very dependable, doing for others, thoughtful of others, kind, doing well and capable. *People should enjoy themselves, too.*

🍃 I am happy, very responsible and do my part of the work.

🍃 I am interested in other people.

🍃 I'm not a manipulator of people. ~~(Perhaps I let them manipulate me?)~~ *I'll stand up for my rights more.*

🍃 Being affectionate and loving is *not always* the best way to go about getting my needs met. *Sometimes I need to assert myself.*

🍃 I'm smart and conscientious.

🍃 I care about others. *and also myself.*

🍃 If you love, you do what others want you to do, *and I also need to do what I want to do.*

🍃 I *am* ~~want to be~~ allowed to do what I want to do.

🍃 It would be nice to be soft and beautiful, very spoiled and well taken care of *so I will take care of myself.*

- I'm torn between my obligation to do for others and my desire to enjoy myself. *I'll consider both in making my decisions.*

- I'm happy doing pleasant things with someone I love.

- *Because*
  ᴀIt's upsetting when people don't fulfill my expectations, *I'll lower my expectations.*

- Life should be a home filled with love, joy and family togetherness.

- *I won't take the weight of the world on my shoulders.*
  ~~I feel bad when anyone else is hurt.~~

- I love having a good time and fun. *I'll make sure I do it.*

- *won't*
  I ᴀfeel guilty when I'm having fun someone else would disapprove of, *as long as I care for both of us.*

- *care*
  I ~~get upset~~ when others are upset.

- *not always*
  Women should ᴀtry to calm men and make them feel better. *It's good for men to solve most of their own problems.*

- ~~Having to wait for joy and celebration makes me impatient and a little angry.~~ *I'm becoming more patient and able to wait. I can always get busy with something else.*

- I handle frustration best by going alone to my room and looking out the window. *(A temporary solution.) But I'll also talk it over with the appropriate person.*

- You should help people *and also yourself.* ~~even if you don't feel like it.~~

A Last Bit
of
Advice

There is one fact of which everyone can be sure—no one is ever going to have all his problems solved, at least not at one time. You get one problem taken care of just in time to begin tackling the next. Most of the time problems overlap. You might find yourself asking, "When does the 'happily ever after' start?"

As I see it, we keep learning things. We finally learn how to change a tire. We ask friends for recipes of particularly luscious casseroles. We discover public libraries have copies of the *Blue Book,* so we can see for ourselves what our cars are worth. We're told what foods will help us live to a ripe old age. The world is full of information and resources we use if we want to be happy.

The mistake many make is waiting for the happiness to come to us. "*Then,* "they think, "I can begin to enjoy life." That's like waiting until you know how to swim before you get into the pool. It will be a long, dry wait.

You need to jump in, flail around and experience your

efforts and mistakes. Little by little, they teach you how to swim easily and well.

Being happy is cultivating the enjoyment of the learning process, even though that process is fraught with swallowed water. Seeing your problems as challenges and opportunities for growth helps you accept them and deal with them in a productive way. Then you can take definite steps in attacking them. You *must* take some kind of action if you want to conquer your problems.

Have you ever been annoyed at a persistent fly that swoops around you, lighting on your nose, your newspaper and your coffee cup? Perhaps you waved it away until finally you realized you'd have to stand up and get the fly-swatter. Many people spend their entire lives "shooing away" problems and never get around to confronting them in a logical, assertive way.

Let me share with you some of my "fly-swatters." These are ways I go about handling the ubiquitous frustrations and discouragements in my life.

Talk

First of all, I talk. (The worst days in my life are when I suffer from laryngitis!) I'm very fortunate to have a husband who listens to me. I constantly bounce ideas off him, looking for his insights. Having adult children is another terrific source of comfort and advice. I talk with them and draw on them frequently. Their personalities are so diverse that each one sees situations with a different approach. I learn from all of them.

Friends

Friends are great providers of fly-swatters! I feel so

lucky to know people like Beth, Joyce, Carolyn, Donna, Virginia, Paula and Wayne. They listen to me with understanding and toss out their ideas for me to consider. Close friends are treasures in our "happiness kits." They usually come to us quite by accident.

We can't look around and choose close friends. They have to develop gradually over time. But we can be open to new acquaintances who will become the strong, bonded, loving friends we can confide in and trust. These people are money in our emotional banks!

We mustn't overlook the pleasure we can find in casual acquaintances, particularly co-workers. We see co-workers frequently; this is fertile ground in which deep, lasting friendships can grow.

People we encounter even briefly often become part of a good support system if we're willing to open up to them. In the years following my mother's death, my father took most of his meals in restaurants around town. The bright spots in his days consisted mostly of smiled greetings and small talk he enjoyed with the waitresses in his favorite cafes. Some of them came to be his loving friends.

What determines who will become close friends? To me, it's evidence of each person's interest in the other. Conversations that are mostly one-sided, with one person doing all the talking, hold little promise. When communication goes both ways in a relatively even exchange, it's a sure sign of friendship!

The only difficulty with seeking advice from friends and family is they love us. They often see situations in exactly the same way we do. They may not be able to help us as effectively as a trained professional with no emotional involvement.

Counselor

Another fly-swatter is the counselor. Sometimes I see a professional counselor and happily pay the fee because I believe in counselors' abilities to see things objectively. A few sessions with a trained counselor or therapist can be the best present you can buy yourself. You go not because you're "sick" but because you deserve to get some help in solving a problem that's understandable to a trained professional. Just as you get an expert to fix your washer or dryer, it makes good sense to get emotional help from experts.

How do you find one? For me, the best source has been talking to friends or acquaintances. People who've been helped by a particular person are usually eager to spread the word. Doctors often recommend counselors or psychologists if we ask. Some may be hesitant to offer a suggestion unsolicited, but they're generally happy to refer a patient who does ask.

Spiritual Advisers

Spiritual advisers are another good fly-swatting source. Many churches and synagogues have clergy who have been trained in counseling. They might also have staff people who are hired for that purpose. If they don't have counselors on staff, they can usually suggest a place to go for help.

Other Sources

There are also thousands of books on self-help and personal growth at our fingertips. Bookstores and libraries are treasures of opportunity. They have books on psychology, children, women, social science, health and religion. All offer a never-ending supply of information and advice. I constantly look for books to present new slants on problems I experience. I learn *something* from almost every book I read.

Classes, workshops and seminars on self-improvement, parenting skills, marriage enrichment, assertiveness, stress management and other topics are available through colleges, parks-and-recreation departments, churches and schools. Another good source of learning is audio tapes by the giants of mental health, such as Wayne Dyer and David Viscott. These tapes are easy to enjoy while you drive, work in the garden or relax in the shade.

Prayer

This book wouldn't be complete without one more suggestion for coping with problems and pain. *Prayer*. I'm sure some of you readers don't believe in God. I don't presume to change your mind. Certainly most books have something in them I don't agree with! But because this is a very personal book, I feel all right in sharing this most personal of all beliefs.

I do believe God answers our prayers. It would be lovely if He answered them exactly the way we ask Him to. But usually He doesn't, as anyone knows who's tried prayer. But I think He knows what He's doing!

Twenty years ago I had so many fears I couldn't count them all. I often prayed God would solve my problems for me and help me be less frightened. I asked Him to help the kids with all their problems, help me get a good night's sleep or whatever.

He didn't.

Or so it seemed. Yet as I look back over the past 20

years and see the help I got from counselors, family, friends and books, there's no question in my mind I got all the help I needed. It seems clear to me now God *did* answer all those prayers. Once a hard-core insomniac, I rarely have trouble sleeping now. My fears are minimal, and most of the time I'm quite delighted with life.

I choose to believe God had a hand in all that.

Sometimes I ask clients if they believe in God. Most of them say they do. But often they add they never go to church anymore. I don't try to get them to do that, but I tell them I believe they can pray without going to church. We can be spiritual in the most unexpected places.

A friend of mine asked his minister, "Is it OK if I smoke while I pray?" He was told, "Probably not. But it's certainly OK if you pray while you smoke."

I pray while I drive, while I cook, while I iron. When I'm in a hurry and I hit a green light, I often say a quick, "Thanks, God!" Not that I presume God sits up there and arranges traffic lights for my convenience, but I'm recognizing Him as a source of all that's good in my life.

It's been interesting to me to see most religious teachings offer the same concepts of "how to be happy" that I teach in counseling. It seems to me mental health and spirituality go hand in hand.

But I don't believe we can sit around lazily, waiting for God to solve our problems. He gave us very capable brains (as well as all these fly-swatting techniques) with which to solve them ourselves. Prayer mustn't take the place of looking for solutions, but it certainly can be included in our self-help skills.

My mother used to recall a tornado that approached Cleveland when she was a little girl. All the neighbors gathered outside to watch the sky and share their fears. My grandmother gathered her children close to her and said firmly, "Pray, kids."

A little neighbor boy standing nearby nuzzled up to Mama's brother John. He said anxiously, "I don't know how to pray, John. Can I hang onto your shirt tail?"

That's faith. You don't have to "know how" to pray nor do you need anyone's shirt tail to hang on to. All you need to do is to talk or think your thoughts to God, to thank Him for so many things and to ask for His help. Then it helps to listen for answers. (Remember, the best friendships are those with nearly equal amounts of talking and listening!)

More things are wrought by prayer than this world dreams of.

For Your Happiness

There you have it—a set of fly-swatters to help you deal with whatever comes down the pike. It's far from complete because you'll keep accumulating new ones all the time if you're in the habit of looking for them.

How freeing it is to realize happiness *is* a do-it-yourself proposition. You don't *have* to make yourself happy. You *get* to do it. What fun it is to use all the methods you can think of to try to achieve happiness. (Or sadness, if you prefer.) The choice is yours.

Here's to happiness—yours!

Dinkmeyer, Don and McKay, Gary, *Raising A Responsible Child*, Simon & Schuster, 1983

Losoncy, Lew, *Turning People On, Prentice Hall, 1977*

Losoncy, Lew, *You Can Do It: How To Encourage Yourself*, Prentice Hall, 1980

Losoncy, Lew and Dinkmeyer, Don, *The Encouragement Book: Becoming A Positive Person*, Prentice Hall, 1980

Low, Abraham, *Mental Health Through Will Training*, Christopher Publishing House, *1971*

Schnebly, Lee, *Out of Apples?*, Fisher Books, 1988

Recovery, Inc.
To find a group near you, contact:
Recovery, Inc.
802 N. Dearborn Street
Chicago, IL 60610
(312) 337-5661

Meetings are free, although they do accept a small donation. A typical Recovery meeting begins with everyone introducing himself by first name, then taking turns reading aloud from a book. Then the leader invites people to tell of some triviality that troubled them recently and how they dealt with it. In a very supportive way, group members examine the incident and offer suggestions and insights, using sentences and phrases that become very familiar and helpful.

Index

A

AA meetings, 61, 113, 150
Achievers, 33, 41, 66, 135, 171, 172
Acting as if, 124-126, 128-129, 148
Addiction, 149-150, 151
Adler, Alfred, 14, 71, 181
Attitudes, 2, 3, 14, 45, 56, 76, 83, 124
    changing, 83
    identifying, 43
    projection, 50-52, 55
    understanding, xiii, 43, 88

B

Behavior, xi-xii, 2-3, 5, 15-16, 20, 24, 26, 27, 28, 32, 34, 42, 44, 46, 49, 60, 76, 77, 79, 80, 82, 84, 115, 117, 126, 131, 135, 136, 141, 162
    changing, 18, 24, 83, 98, 118, 121, 124, 126, 129, 137
    new, 80, 117, 124, 129
Belief System, 1-3, 5, 15, 26, 71, 73, 78, 79
Beliefs, 1-2, 4, 5, 6, 7, 8, 38, 64, 66, 68-69, 73, 74, 77, 79, 83-85, 88, 98-99, 105, 107-110, 114, 117, 118, 128, 138, 182, 195
    changing, 4, 8, 9, 80, 83, 84, 107, 108, 109, 110, 117-118, 129, 135
    childhood, 5
    conflicting, 73
    determining, 9
    identifying, 43, 114, 115
    mistaken, 4, 6, 8, 74, 80, 161
    new, 8, 84, 110, 112, 121, 145, 157, 169, 179, 188
        creating, 8, 80, 84

old, 3, 121, 156, 167, 177, 186
    understanding, xiii, 29, 73
    unrealistic, 110
Birth order, 13, 14, 17, 24, 25, 26, 28, 29, 89
    firstborn, 8, 14-18, 24, 26-27
    middle child, 19-20, 24, 26-27
    only child, 23-25, 28
    second child, 15-19, 24, 26
    youngest child, 20-23, 25-26
Bobbsey Twins, the, 183

C

Change, xi, xii, 2, 3, 4, 8-10, 40, 60-61, 64, 68, 77, 80, 83-84, 89, 98, 107, 108-109, 117-118, 121, 129-130, 135, 137
    ability to, 43
    courage to, 61, 123-126, 128, 129
    willingness to, 3, 4, 6, 40, 43, 66, 68, 98, 108, 117, 149
Changing the past, 11, 59-61, 80-81, 83, 85, 90-91, 102, 141, 153, 164, 175, 184
Changing the present, 11, 61, 84-85, 91, 102, 107, 108, 110, 118, 141, 153, 164, 173, 175, 184
Charmers, 22, 25, 135, 148-150
Childhood, xi-xii, 3, 5, 10-12, 14, 32-35, 38-39, 41-43, 46-47, 59, 61, 63, 65- 69, 76, 79, 80, 82, 89-91, 101-102, 118, 136, 139, 140-141, 151-153, 160-164, 172-175, 182-184
Christensen, Dr. Oscar, 18-20
Cinderella, 52
Communication, 107, 138, 172, 193
Communicators, 40, 44
Competition, 16-19, 24, 26, 65
Compliments, 11, 40-42, 65, 90,